PRESIDENTIAL PLUNGE

THEODORE ROOSEVELT, THE PLUNGER SUBMARINE, & THE UNITED STATES NAVY

Adam M. Grohman

Also by Adam M. Grohman

Non-Fiction

Non Liquet
The Bayville Submarine Mystery

Runner Aground
A History of the Schooner *William T. Bell*

Ugly Duckling
Liberty Ship *S.S. C.W. Post*

Mask, Fins & Knife
A History of the U.S. Navy UDT & SEAL
Diving Equipment from World War II to Present

Beneath the Blue & Gray Waves
Sub-Marine Warfare of the American Civil War

Claimed by the Sea
Long Island Shipwrecks

Non–Fiction with Andrew Campbell

Dive GTMO
Scuba Diving in Guantanamo Bay, Cuba

Fiction

A Bright Shining Light

Surfer Girl – A Love Story

168

PRESIDENTIAL PLUNGE
Theodore Roosevelt, the *Plunger* Submarine
and the United States Navy

Adam M. Grohman
ISBN # 978-0-578-03122-4

Dedication

This book and research is dedicated to my brother-in-law Ryan Vessichelli, Ensign, United States Navy. May he and his fellow shipmates continue the legacy of proud service to the United States Navy and the citizens of both the United States and the world.

This research is also dedicated to my sons, Aidan and Liam. May they grow up to learn and appreciate the importance and value of education and knowledge.

Acknowledgements

Though my initial plan was to dip into the brief history of Theodore Roosevelt's submarine voyage for a short graduate school project, I soon found myself immersed in an amazing historical legacy of support not only for the submarine service, but the U.S. Navy as a whole. The short paper evolved quickly, especially as I dove deeper and deeper into a more adventurous project. Multiple reviews of details during the research process to attempt to determine fact from fiction often resulted in long nights, thus keeping me from the cozy confines and the silence of slumber. Finally however, after several years, I was able to surface from my trip into history, having completed a definitive history of Theodore Roosevelt, the *Plunger* Submarine and the United States Navy.

Ultimately, the research and final volume would not have been possible without the support of the following persons and organizations: Capt. Don T. Sine, U.S.N. Retired, for reviewing multiple drafts of the research, Commander Henry J. Hendrix, U.S.N., for offering his insight and an introduction to the final draft; Ms. Kim McKeithan of the National Archives, Old War Records Division, for locating the original deck logs for the *U.S.S.T.B. Plunger*, library staff members of the Long Island University, C.W. Post Campus, and the public libraries located in Locust Valley, Glen Cove, and Oyster Bay, New York; to the members and supporters of the Underwater Historical Research Society who continue to advocate for the mission to Research – Identify – Educate. Lastly and most importantly, I would like to extend my thanks and appreciation to my wife Kendall, sons Aidan and Liam, and my parents and in-laws, for their patience and understanding over the past two years as I dove into the archives to bring Roosevelt's historic submarine adventure to the surface.

Table of Contents

Introduction

Since George Washington took the oath of office as our nation's first chief executive, no less than 23 of the 44 men who have led our nation have served in the United States Army, 12 of them achieving the rank of general officer. Twenty two of these men served prior to 1961 (Ronald Reagan is the only Army officer to go on to the Presidency since Dwight Eisenhower left office). By and large the strategic outlook that these men gained from their experiences as ground force commanders served them well during their presidencies. They exhibited a strong focus on conquering the North American continent during the 19th century, and defending American interests in Europe and Asia during the 20th century. However, it was those presidents who hailed from a naval background who truly ushered in the expansion of American power over the past one hundred years. Beginning with the Roosevelts, Theodore and his distant cousin Franklin, each of whom served as Assistant Secretary of the Navy, and then proceeding through Kennedy, Lyndon Johnson, Nixon, Ford, Carter, and George H.W. Bush, each of these men approached the world from a decidedly naval perspective and the ships of the Navy and the men of the Marine Corps were their principle tools of persuasion. Looking back over these men and their records, it is clear that no one mastered the intricacies of naval operations more thoroughly than Theodore Roosevelt.

Theodore Roosevelt was a multi-faceted individual. His interests ranged from the natural world, to historical literature, from national defense to government reform. It is difficult to understand him to any degree of certainty when you choose to look at him from only one lens of analysis, and yet that is what modern historians often try to do with figures of the past. The study of history, it has been decided by the professionals, is simply too broad for any one person to master, and so the profession has begun to guide each successive generation of PhD's into lanes of greater and greater specialization; ancient history, military history, diplomatic history, and technological history to name a few of the new categories that subdivide the shelves of the local bookstore.

Thankfully Adam Grohman is not a PhD, but is in fact a genuine human being who is marked by the same love of the fullness of life that characterized Theodore Roosevelt's time upon this planet. Husband, father, student, author, diver and Coast Guardsman who has served his country in its moment of need, he has demonstrated much of that same frenetic energy that caused one of Roosevelt's contemporaries to label him as a creature of "pure act," and that is not a bad thing at all. Because of his background, and because he has never been inhibited by the type of professional instruction that would tell him what he cannot do, Mr. Grohman has produced a remarkable book that centers upon one event, but then spins the reader three hundred and sixty degrees around the focal point to discover the interconnected nature, the "wholeness" of Theodore Roosevelt's life, his interest in the Navy and its impact upon the United States at the dawn of the 20th Century.

Theodore Roosevelt and the United States Navy; the United States Navy and Theodore Roosevelt. One cannot be reasonably understood without considering and factoring in the impact of the other. Theodore Roosevelt is the father of the modern American Navy, and as the modern Navy is a critical "keystone" component of the United States' rise to Great Power Status over the past century, one can accurately state that birth of the "American Century" occurred during Theodore Roosevelt's administration. For its part, the United States Navy has never forgotten T.R.. If the reader has a calendar that shows all of the nation's commemorative holidays (as opposed to just those you get the day off from work for) you will discover that "Navy Day" is celebrated each year on October 27th, which is not coincidentally, Theodore Roosevelt's birthday. Sailors still remember who we have to thank for the fleet we sail to the far corners of the world, following in the wake of T.R.'s Great White Fleet. So the question becomes: what must we take away from a small incident in which a sitting president briefly submerged in a submarine?

Everything. Grand Strategy, small unit tactics, technological research and development, grooming and growing the enlisted and officer corps, its all there. Grohman utilizes Theodore Roosevelt's brief sojourn beneath the waters off of his home at Oyster Bay, NY as a Rosetta Stone to segue and translate the various, seemingly disparate themes of T.R.'s life into a coherent whole. From his childhood listening to stories of the sea as told by his mother, to his time at Harvard and beyond in the early years of his professional life as a writer, Mr. Grohman presents a view of Roosevelt's interest in the Navy as a constantly evolving, central theme of his life. While some might study Roosevelt's presidency from the vantage point of the success of his diplomacy (after all, he did receive the Nobel Peace Prize) and another might study Roosevelt's life as an example of militant belligerency (and then again he was a recipient of the Medal of Honor), Adam Grohman both senses and conveys that Roosevelt's military and foreign policies are two parts of one whole national strategy. That it was the first coherent strategy for our republic is only now being recognized and appreciated.

Roosevelt had latched onto the Monroe Doctrine, which had languished for nearly seventy-five years, as the central pillar of his own outlook on the world early in his public career. Whether he needed this idea of establishing virtual American suzerainty in the western hemisphere to justify his large Navy, or whether he desired the Navy to support the Monroe Doctrine has become a source of a "chicken or the egg" academic discussion, but regardless the net effect was that Roosevelt at first blocked European interference in the Western Hemisphere, and then established a "sphere of influence" in the traditional form with the United States as the unquestioned leader on the American continents. He did this with strong consistent foreign policy statements that were in turn backed by an evolutionary naval building plan that saw the United States Navy

8

move from seventh in the world in terms of gross tonnage to a position second only to Great Britain. He also championed technological advancement that saw the rise of the all big gun battleship, destroyers, aviation, and, of course, submarines.

Theodore Roosevelt has been gone in his physical form for 90 years but his ideas still speak to those who would listen. Adam Grohman has been listening, and the story he has to tell is a compelling one. I commend him for his efforts and invite the reader to take the time to fully consider the implications of the words he has written. Within them one can discern the blueprint for the American 20th Century, and while this master plan did not begin with a short voyage on a small submarine, it is certainly exemplified by that journey.

Henry J. Hendrix II
Commander, USN (PhD)
The Pentagon, Washington DC
28 May 2009

Author's Preface

Over a century has passed since Lieutenant Nelson ventured up the pathway of Sagamore Hill to see if President Theodore Roosevelt wished to take an adventure on board the submarine boat *Plunger*. My son Aidan and I are walking along the same path. It is an early morning in July and the summer's heat has yet to dry the dew from the freshly cut grass of the grounds. A few visitors wait patiently for a National Park Ranger to provide a tour of the Roosevelt home. AJ and I however, have already been on the tour on a previous visit to the national park, so we decide to take a walk on the grounds instead. I try to imagine how the young United States Navy lieutenant felt as he walked up to the covered porch of the house to knock on the door.

Sagamore Hill National Park. Author's collection.

We continue on our self guided tour and visit the old orchard house, former home of Theodore Roosevelt Jr., which is located on the same property and now houses a museum.[1] We are the only two visitors so we take a slow chronological journey through President Theodore Roosevelt's life. There is mention of Teddy Roosevelt's legacy in regards to the United States Navy and

---

[1] Son of Theodore Roosevelt and a United States Army General who landed at D-Day on Utah Beach.

naval supremacy, but there is no mention of his historic submarine adventure in any detail. To find out more, I would have to investigate various sources and research facilities.

We finish our walk and chatted with a young park ranger named Tom. We discuss the *Plunger* trip and he suggests that I contact the head curator of the site. In addition, AJ is lucky enough to be "deputized" as a Junior National Park Ranger and he even received his very own gold Department of the Interior badge. I thanked Tom and AJ waved goodbye.

As we drove down the driveway (added later as a service entrance for deliveries), I looked back at Sagamore Hill. We drove down the hill and the secluded waters of Oyster Bay quickly came into view. I pulled the truck over to the side of the road and looked out upon the crystal serene waters. Not much had changed and I could almost imagine President Roosevelt heading out on a small launch to board the *Plunger* for this historic trip.

Aidan Jack Grohman, my son, helping me with my research. Author's collection.

As I would eventually learn from my research, his ride on the submarine was more than just another adventure. Rather, the submarine trip was just one example of Roosevelt's steadfast support of the United States Navy and an illustration of a lifelong dedication to the seagoing service. The support provided by Roosevelt, throughout his life, to the United States Navy assisted in the foundation of today's modern fleet. In that capacity, his support continues to be visibly represented as just one of the many Roosevelt's contributions to the United States and the World.

Adam M. Grohman
Chief Diver and Researcher
Underwater Historical Research Society
Sagamore Hill National Park
Summer 2007

Introduction - Syllogism & the Gray Haze of Historical Research

The Greek philosopher Aristotle identified the concept of formal logic and explained that it existed based on a number of rules used to insure the logical accuracy of statements. Three aspects made up the concept, including the major premise, minor premise and a conclusion. The major premise was a general statement that was known to be true from observation. The minor premise was another statement that utilized one of the terms of the major premise but referred to a single aspect. Lastly, the conclusion was based on the remaining terms of the major and minor premise. According to Walter T. K. Nugent's book, *Creative History, An Introduction to Historical Research*, formal logic "dealt much more adequately with statements that were only probable or conjectural." (Nugent, 138) He continued by stating that "of course, nearly all statements in history, except the most badly factual ones, are only probable or conjecture." (Nugent, 138)

So the real question raised by his "premise" is whether or not the concept of syllogism is applicable to historical research. Nugent argues that the concept of probable or conjectural statements do not "remove history from the realm of logic" but rather that "historical statements are not often black-and-white, absolutely certain or absolutely false. They are almost always some shade of gray." (Nugent, 138)

I have pondered this concept of probable and conjectural statements and its relation to formal logic throughout my research on the *U.S.S. Plunger* and President Theodore "Teddy" Roosevelt's historic dive below the murky waves of the Long Island Sound.[2] Much of what I have found is probable and conjectural. Much of what occurred that day in August 1905 has been lost or the few facts

---

[2] Roosevelt was the first United States President to descend beneath the waves in a submarine boat; however he was not the first head of state to complete such a daring feat. "President Emile Loubet of France had claimed that distinction in 1901." (Parrish, 34)

that do remain have been expounded upon erroneously either on purpose for dramatic effect or by simple mistake.

But whether conjectural or probable, one truth is apparent. President Roosevelt's brief dip into the abyss on the revolutionary and dangerous undersea boat provided a foundation for acceptance of the strange underwater crafts by not only the government but also the United States Navy. Most importantly, his "adventure" in the abyss would prove to be vital to the development of the United States Naval Submarine service and to the men and women who comprise this arm of the United States Naval fleet to this day. But his trip under the waves on board the *Plunger* is only one of many examples of how Roosevelt supported the United States Navy throughout his lifetime. Hopefully my research will provide that his legacy for the submarine service and the United States Navy in general, not be lost as have the details of his brief, yet very important submarine adventure.

Chapter 1 - Orders and Anticipation

The order had been sent to the Brooklyn Navy Yard for the *U.S.S. Plunger*, under command of United States Navy Lieutenant Charles Preston Nelson, to report for a review for President Theodore Roosevelt.[3] The orders, forwarded from the Secretary of the Navy read, "You are to proceed as soon as possible to Oyster Bay and report to the President."

The *Plunger* submarine. Author's collection.

But according to the article titled, "President May Take Dip - Submarine Called For," that appeared in the *Daily Northwestern*'s evening edition, was that when "the orders came the boat was in dry dock being overhauled." Immediately, however, the submarine torpedo boat was placed in the water and a "large force of expert engineers and merchants" began diligent work, both day and night to get "the little craft into shape." Much work had to be completed as "an entire set of new and heavily insulated electric light wires" as well as another gasoline engine was being overhauled and "revamped."

---

[3] Lieutenant Nelson's nickname, according to author Hermann Hagedorn was "Daredevil Nelson." (Hagedorn, 227)

It was obvious to the casual observer that no chances were going to be taken with the president and the submarine. According to articles published in the *Daily-Northwestern*, *The Fort Wayne Evening Sentinel*, and the *Oakland Tribune*, every precaution was being taken to provide a smooth "sailing" and a safe trip if the President decided to go aboard the craft. In the *Oakland Tribune*'s article, titled, "President May Dive," every single "bolt and rivet is being subjected to a thorough resodering and the torpedo tube is being frequently tested."

But it would be another five days or so before Lieutenant Nelson, his crew, and his craft would be ready to ship out in accordance to their orders. The day and nights were spent drilling, painting, soldering, checking and re-checking every square inch from bulkhead to bulkhead, frame to frame.

The real question that was raised in the various articles and that rested on everyone's mind was whether or not President Roosevelt would in fact take the plunge onboard the submarine torpedo boat. In the *Fort Wayne Sentinel*, "although it is said that the President has several times expressed a desire to go down in a submarine, and the officers of the *Plunger* are extremely anxious to have the Chief executive as their guest dip below the water's surface, no intimation of such a plan has been given, and the men admit that they expect only to show the president how their craft works." Only time would tell. Lieutenant Nelson however, could not allow his hand picked crew or the various engineers or mechanics to spend any time focusing in on the possibility of the president going beneath the surface of the waves. He had to instead keep them focused on the monumental task at hand. The fate of the United States Naval Submarine force lay on the shoulders of one man and one boat.

A few days later, the front page of the August 13, 1905 Sunday edition of the *Washington Post* provided an update for all of the world's events. Under the title, "Lodge at Oyster Bay," an update was provided regarding the upcoming "Tests of the Plunger." According to the *Washington Post*, the tests of the submarine boat were to take place within a week or ten days, but that the "arrangements for the test," had not yet been completely determined. In the meanwhile, the *U.S.S. Plunger* continued its overhaul and preparation for its trip to the waters of Oyster Bay. "Her commander," referring to Nelson, "is recognized in the navy as one of the most fearless and accomplished officers in the service." The pressure was certainly on the young officer as "his record attracted the attention of President Roosevelt who gave directions that Lieut. Nelson should come to Oyster Bay in the *U.S.S. Plunger* in order that he might have the opportunity to witness personally the practical performance of the vessel."

The real question of whether or not the President would actually go on or down was squashed as according to the report, it was stated that the "President has no thought of being aboard the *Plunger* during the tests." But the President was however, quick to point out that his decision was based on "no fear of possible mishap, but he believes that he could achieve no good result by being onboard the vessel while tests are in progress, and, in fact that he simply would be in the way." Instead the Commander in Chief would simply observe the tests from the tranquility and safety of the presidential yacht *Sylph*.[4] Thousands of New Yorkers on their way to work on the morning of August 19, 1905 might have missed the small one paragraph mention of the upcoming "Tests of the Plunger." The snippet or mention of the upcoming event was on page three.

---

[4] The *Sylph* would return Roosevelt to Sagamore Hill after the President and three men, including a secret service agent named Craig, were involved in a terrible accident. The carriage the men were riding in was struck by a trolley, killing the secret service agent and threw Roosevelt "thirty feet onto the pavement." Roosevelt completed his scheduled speaking engagement and then returned from Bridgeport. Roosevelt was reported to have been saddened by the loss of the "burly, blue-eyed Scot" who had become a dear friend to not only Roosevelt, but also to his children. (Hagedorn, 166)

17

Holland submarines of the U.S. Navy. Author's collection.

According to the article, tentative arrangements had been made to have the "submarine torpedo boat *Plunger*," provide President Theodore Roosevelt with a demonstration of her abilities at the entrance of Oyster Bay the following Wednesday. The article also introduced the readers of the *New York Times* with the commanding officer, Lieutenant Charles Nelson, who would provide the leadership for the demonstration.[5] The *U.S.S. Plunger*, according to the article was to arrive in Oyster Bay on the twenty-first or twenty-second of August to prepare for the President's review.

The *U.S.S. Plunger* was an *Adder* class submarine and was only four years old when she was summoned to the waters of Oyster Bay, Long Island, New York, for her presidential review. The submarine torpedo boat, *A-1, SS-2* was the first of the *Adder* class. Her predecessor was the *U.S.S. Holland*[6] and the

---

[5] Most readers of the paper probably missed a small previous mention of Nelson in an April 17, 1904 article. See *Appendix A* for more information.

[6] The *U.S.S. Plunger* should not be confused with the previous Holland submarine named *Plunger* that was powered by a steam engine. Though successful in its operation, the use of steam-power was not conducive for submarine boats.

Adder was the first of the initially delivered functional submarines for the United States Naval Fleet after improvements had been made to the *U.S.S. Holland, SS-1* of the *Holland* class design. The submarine boats of the *Adder* class, of which there would be a total of seven, represented a new technology that had been "somewhat" perfected by submarine designer and inventor John Holland.

The *U.S.S. Plunger*'s keel was laid on May 21, 1901 at Crescent Shipyards in Elizabethport, New Jersey. She was launched on February 1, 1902 and was commissioned the *U.S.S. Plunger* on September 19, 1903 at the Holland Company docks in New Suffolk, Long Island, New York. The *U.S.S. Plunger* was sixty-three feet, ten inches long with a beam of eleven feet, eleven inches. She drafted ten feet, seven inches, and displaced one hundred and seven tons on the surface and one hundred and twenty-three tons submerged. She was propelled through the water by a single screw or propeller which was attached to an Otto Gas Engine Works gasoline engine. For underwater operation, she was supplied with Electro Dynamic electric motors that generated one hundred and fifty horsepower and had a complement of sixty battery cells. The 160 horsepower engine allowed the submarine to speed along the surface at eight knots and seven knots while submerged. The *U.S.S. Plunger*'s complement of crew was as small as the boat, with one officer and six enlisted men working the operation of the submerging craft.

On August 19, 1905, the crew of the *U.S.S. Plunger* prepared for her presidential review in the waters of the Long Island Sound. The crew and officer in charge, Lieutenant Charles Nelson must have been very excited at the opportunity to showcase the new craft for President Roosevelt and worked diligently to clean and prepare the submarine. The *U.S.S. Plunger*, however, had different plans. The article on page two of the August 22, 1905 *New York Times* newspaper highlighted the inherent problem with the *U.S.S. Plunger*'s date with the President. "Defect In The Plunger – Machinery Almost Red-Hot When Tested For Oyster Bay Trip." Frustration had set in as Lieutenant Nelson had

19

stated "disgustedly that he did not know when she would get away." Under his supervision, the *U.S.S. Plunger* had undergone tests prior to its planned departure for Oyster Bay when she had begun to experience problems with her machinery. However, Nelson explained to the reporter that "We are going to work all night though, and hope to get out to-morrow morning."

A Holland submarine. Author's collection.

The "trouble" was with the submarine's electrical apparatus which was not functioning properly. During one of the tests, 1,100 amperes were being shown when the normal ampere load should not have been more then 500. This additional amperage was neither expected nor safe for the undersea craft and further examination and overhauling needed to be completed prior to her leaving the pier.

The submarine remained tied up to the pier "just beyond the big battleship Connecticut," which according to the article looked "like a real man-of-war, her three massive funnels having been just put in place." Nelson supervised two civilian electrical engineers who with hard work, "expected to find out exactly what was wrong, and hoped to be able to pronounce the *U.S.S. Plunger* safe enough for even a President of the United States to venture in" by the morning.

The *U.S.S. Plunger* was not a new boat, but the technology certainly was. Even though submarines had been used in conflicts prior, including the Civil War, the submarine was still a very dangerous invention.[7] The then recent disasters of the British Submarine *A-1* and the French Submarine *Farfadet* must have played on Lieutenant Nelson's nerves as he prepped the submarine for her trip to Oyster Bay.[8] To provide an additional level of safety, "six steel eyes, each of which can hold a massive hawser," were fitted to the hull of the submarine. The *U.S.S. Plunger* had made over three hundred submerged trips, but the upcoming review by the President was paramount for not only the fledgling United States Navy Submarine Fleet but also for Lieutenant Nelson's career. "I do not know exactly why we have been ordered to Oyster Bay," Nelson explained, "but I imagine the President wants to keep in touch with the improvements being made in this branch of the service." Nelson went on to say that he wished that "Mr. Roosevelt would down with us, but whether he will or not is a different question."

---

[7] Nelson did not want any problems with the voyage to Oyster Bay. Roughly seven months earlier, on January 23, 1905, the submarine "came near sinking at her dock at the torpedo station" in Newport, Rhode Island. (*NYT*, 24JAN1905) The taking on of water "was the result of a sea valve having been left open. It was noticed that the submarine was very low, and investigation showed two feet of water in the hold." (*NYT*, 24JAN1905) The torpedo boat *McKee* rendered assistance and the submarine was inspected for any damage incurred by the flooding sea water.

[8] The *Farfadet*, a French submarine sank on July 6, 1905, only a month before the first word of the President's possible dip beneath the waves. The *Farfadet* sank to the bottom at the entrance of the port of Sidi Abdallah, Tunis with a crew of fourteen men. Though attempts were made to save the submarine and her crew, all efforts failed. The *Farfadet* was finally recovered on July 15, 1905. On July 7th, 1905, with the crew still alive and tapping on the hull, the submarine had been raised by cables to the surface. Before the crew was able to escape to the safety of the surface, the cables holding the submarine snapped, plunging the submarine to the bottom. (*NYT*, 7JUL and 16JUL1905) Five subsequent efforts were unsuccessful in raising the submarine and saving her crew. The British *A-1*, the former *Holland #6* was "rammed and sunk by steamship *Berwick Castle*, March 18, 1904, off Nab Tower, Portsmouth," with the loss of her entire crew. (Hutchinson, 35) Sadly, her sister ship, *A-3* was lost in the "same way in almost the same position – rammed and sunk by the aptly named submarine tender – *HMS Hazard* – off the Isle of Wright on February 2, 1912, again with all crew lost." (Hutchinson, 35)

So as the article appeared on page two of the *New York Times*, Nelson, his enlisted crew, and the civilian electrical engineers continued to trouble shoot the electrical malfunction. The United States Navy Tugboat *Apache* waited at an adjacent pier awaiting word of the submarine's successful test. The *Apache* stood by to tow the *U.S.S. Plunger* through the waters of New York to the summer waters of the Long Island Sound. Once into the calm waters of the Long Island Sound the *Apache* would head eastward to Oyster Bay and to the President of the United States.

Chapter 2 - Theodore Roosevelt

Theodore Roosevelt became the twenty-sixth president of the United States after the assassination of President William McKinley. For many, the presidency of the United States would be the pinnacle of success, but for Theodore Roosevelt it as just one of his many accomplishments. After taking the oath of office he began his reign as the Commander-in-Chief of the United States.

President Roosevelt. Author's collection.

Roosevelt was born the second of four children to Theodore Roosevelt Sr. and Mittie Bulloch. He was born on October 27, 1858 and spent the majority of his childhood in sickness. *Teedie* as he was nicknamed as a child was fascinated at an early age in the study of animals. By nine years of age he had written a paper regarding his insect investigation titled the *Natural History of Insects*. Researching and writing would mark a trend that would exist for the majority of his life.

Roosevelt was home schooled by his parents and tutors and though his education was sometimes uneven in its coverage of subjects, he matriculated at Harvard in 1876. He graduated magna cum laude in 1880 and entered Columbia Law School, but dropped out one year later in an attempt to secure a seat in the New York State Assembly. Though the Roosevelt household had originally been Democrats, the family had converted politically to the Republican Party in the mid 1850's. As an assemblyman, Roosevelt was an active legislator and wrote more bills then any other New York State assemblymen.

At twenty-two, Roosevelt married Alice Hathaway Lee. Two years later, a daughter Alice was born. During this same time frame, Roosevelt finished writing his history of the naval war of 1812. But tragedy soon followed and both his wife and mother died on Valentine's Day, 1884. Roosevelt left the New York State Assembly, left his daughter in the care and custody of his older sister and headed west to Dakota Territory.

In the Badlands, Roosevelt lived as a rancher and lawman. While recovering from the loss of his wife, Roosevelt wrote frontier life stories for magazines, learned how to ride horses, hunt, and rope. He was a deputy sheriff and was quite successful in his law enforcement activities but after his cattle were wiped out in the winter of 1886-1887, Roosevelt returned to New York. He purchased Sagamore Hill and ran for the Mayor of New York City. He did not win.

After his loss in the mayoral race, Roosevelt traveled to London and married Edith Kermit Carow. He continued to write, completing biographies of Thomas Hart Benton in 1887 and Gouverneur Morris in 1888, and more importantly, he wrote *The Winning of the West*, which was a four volume history of the expansion westward, which was completed between 1889 and 1896. The major work, coupled with is previous book regarding the naval war of 1812, solidified Roosevelt's contribution as a historian. *The Winning of the West* also showcased Roosevelt's concept that the expansion west had created a new race or people called Americans. Roosevelt had utilized the Lamarkean scientific model to support his interpretations stating that a new environment had allowed a new species to form.

Though he had achieved literary success, he still campaigned heavily. In 1888 he supported Benjamin Harrison and upon Harrison's election, Roosevelt was appointed to the United States Civil Service Commission, a post he maintained until 1895. During his service to both Harrison and Grover Cleveland, Roosevelt worked diligently to demand the enforcement of civil service. Roosevelt would take this same tenacious work ethic to his next position as the President of the New York City Board of Police Commissioners. He and his fellow board members established new disciplinary rules, standardized annual physical exams, and 32 caliber pistol practices for all of the officers. 1,600 additional officers were appointed based on merit, as opposed to the previously utilized political-based system, and for the first time, minorities and women were provided open admission to the New York Police Department. An energetic and forward thinking leader, Roosevelt soon became embroiled in many public disagreements with his superiors. This would be a pattern that would continue as he moved up the political ladder.

Under the urging of Congressman Henry Cabot Lodge, President William McKinley appointed Roosevelt as the Assistant Secretary of the Navy in 1897, under the proviso that Roosevelt would do as he was told and not to ruffle too many feathers. But during his brief tenure at the post, Roosevelt continued to advocate for a strong navy and his enthusiasm for a practical test of the U.S. military soon came with the explosion of the battleship *U.S.S. Maine* in Havana Harbor and the start of the Spanish-American War. After providing leadership as the acting secretary as his superior was on vacation, Roosevelt took another step to enter the war more individually, by offering his resignation. With the assistance of Colonel Leonard Wood, Roosevelt organized the First U.S. Volunteer Calvary Regiment which would later be referred to as the "Rough Riders."

Successful campaigns during the war would lead Roosevelt to the national forefront as an American Hero. Upon his return to politics, Roosevelt was elected Governor of New York on the Republican ticket and was chosen as McKinley's running mate for the 1900 presidential election. The uneventful first months of his vice-presidency were shattered when President McKinley was shot on September 14, 1901 by Leon Czolgoszan, an anarchist.

Roosevelt's two terms as President were quite eventful. He proposed the "Square Deal" concept which became his anti-trust campaign, passed the Hepburn Act of 1906 which granted the interstate Commerce Commission to regulate maximum railroad rates, was an active environmental conservationist, and supported preservation of historic landmarks and other objects of historic or scientific relevance with the Antiquities Act of 1906.

Roosevelt's two terms were also paramount as he actively pursued and initiated foreign policy. One instrument was his addition to the Monroe Doctrine of his "Roosevelt Corollary" which stated that the United States could intervene in Latin American Affairs when corruption was apparent. The Roosevelt Corollary was followed by the support to build the Panama Canal which would take over ten years of U.S. efforts to be completed.

After his second administration, Roosevelt remained in the public eye and was never far from the forefront. He continued his political involvement, traveled extensively on safaris collecting thousands of specimens for use in museums, created the Progressive Party which was coined the "Bull Moose" party, was shot by a disgruntled saloon keeper, John Schrank in 1912 as he was campaigning. Interestingly enough, Roosevelt's steel eyeglass case and a copy of the speech slowed down the impact of the bullet and though many suggested that he go to the hospital, Roosevelt gave his ninety minute speed, with the bullet lodged in his chest.[9] The bullet would remain in his chest for the rest of his life.

All throughout his post presidency years, Roosevelt continued to explore, write, support scientific research, offer political opinions, and support the Boy Scouts of America. On January 6, 1919, at the age of sixty, Roosevelt passed away in his sleep of a coronary embolism.

The man who had advocated for the "strenuous life" and had worn many hats – politician, writer, lawman, naval secretary, civil service commissioner, rough rider, vice president, president, scientist, explorer, environmental conservationist- had passed away. But his legacy in virtually all of the fields that he ventured remains significant to this day, especially his legacy regarding the United States Navy.

---

[9] Roosevelt completed the speech in Milwaukee and did not see a surgeon regarding the injury until he reached Chicago via train. "The surgeon decided not to operate given the risk of anesthesia, infection, and surgical mortality." The bullet had lodged between his fourth rib "but [that it] had not entered the chest cavity." Therefore, the surgeon "gave Roosevelt a tetanus shot, bandaged his chest and ordered him on bed rest for several days." (Blank-Reid, 32)

Chapter 3 - In Oyster Bay

By six o'clock on the evening of August 22, 1905, the *U.S.S. Plunger* had arrived and was anchored in the outer bay of Oyster Bay Harbor. She lay just "astern of the Presidential yacht *Sylph*." According to the article, again on page one of the *New York Times*, on August 23, 1905, the submarine's travel to Oyster Bay was "without mishap or incident. She was convoyed by the naval tug *Apache*, aboard which the *U.S.S. Plunger*'s crew of eight will bunk and board."

Lieutenant Nelson, the two civilian electrical engineers, and the *U.S.S. Plunger*'s enlisted crewmen had worked through the night and day of the twenty first to make the trip a success. Off of Fort Schuyler, the *U.S.S. Plunger* cast off from the *U.S.S. Apache*'s tow line and had entered Oyster Bay under her own power, beating the tug. Overall, Lieutenant Nelson must have felt that it was quite a successful trip but the true test would come with the President's inspection. A day or more was still required to prepare and "groom their boat and make other necessary arrangements before she can show off her qualities to advantage."

The future of the submarine service in a way, rested in the hands of Lieutenant Nelson and the crew of the submarine. Presidential support for the fledgling aspect of the naval service would provide the ability for the submarines and her crews to continue to push the boats, the technology, and explore the future of the submarine torpedo boats for coastal defense and offensive strategies. According to the article "President Roosevelt had "not yet decided when he will inspect the naval craft," so Lieutenant Nelson had to prepare his boat and be ready at a moments notice.

By the next day however, the *U.S.S. Plunger* took its first submerged run in the waters of Oyster Bay for the "purpose of trying out her machinery and tuning up for her test exhibition before the President." (*NYT*, 24AUG1905) According to the page two article titled, "Sees the Plunger Dive," Nelson and his crew completed various maneuvers in the waters off of the Seawanhaka-

28

Corinthian Yacht Club landing while "Mrs. Roosevelt, accompanied by Miss Ethel Roosevelt and Archie and Quentin, two of the President's younger sons," looked on while onboard the presidential yacht *Sylph*'s motor launch, the *Dart*.

But where was the President? "According to a statement given out at the executive office to-day her exhibition drill for the benefit of President Roosevelt will not occur until Friday or Saturday." In addition, the President dispelled any rumors of a possible trip underwater on board the submarine. As the day drew to a close, Lieutenant Nelson must have been proud of his crew, but disappointed that the President did not plan on taking a trip below the waves onboard the *U.S.S. Plunger*. But as the late August sun set in the west, Nelson did not know what the next sunrise would bring and onboard the *U.S.S. Apache*, the crew remained awaiting news of the President's pending review.

The time for the tests of the submarine for the President however, did not necessarily rest in the fate of the President, as the time for the tests had "not yet been decided upon, as it is the President's intention this shall be fixed to suit the convenience of Mrs. Roosevelt, who is as anxious as the President to witness the performance." So the time was not known, but the date of Saturday, August 25, 1905 was determined as the day for the presidential review.

The crew of the submarine started early on the morning of the 24th painting over the submarine's black finish with coat of fresh vivid green paint. The torpedo boat remained moored along side the *U.S.S. Apache*. As the preparations continued, Lieutenant Nelson was informed that he had been summoned to the summer White House, Sagamore Hill, to meet with the President.

Over a luncheon at Sagamore Hill, "the plans for the exhibition of the *Plunger*'s qualities were then talked over by the President and Lieut. Nelson." The plan for the exhibition was that "the President and Mrs. Roosevelt and a party of guests will witness the manoeuvres from the deck of the naval yacht *Sylph*," which lay at the ready at an anchorage in the outer bay.

The *Plunger* –possibly in Oyster Bay? Courtesy of the National Archives.

Upon his return to the *U.S.S. Plunger*, Nelson must have been full of energy as he knew the next day that the President of the United States and his guests would be on scene to view the submarine as she displayed her abilities. But could the president sit idle onboard his yacht *Sylph* as the undersea boat ran through its sea trials? Wouldn't a more adventurous time be had going under with the crew in the submarine boat? Only time would tell for both Nelson and the President.[10]

---

[10] It is quite possible that both men already knew the answer to the question. According to Hermann Hagedorn's version of events, as outlined in *The Roosevelt Family of Sagamore Hill*, "when the young commander reported at Sagamore Hill the President told him: 'I'm going down in your boat, but please don't say anything about it. When it is all over, it'll be time to talk about it." (Hagedorn, 227)

Chapter 4 - The Submarine

The tenets of submarine or submersible craft have changed little since the idea was first originated. Submersible crafts utilize the concept of Archimedes principle which states "that a body immersed in a fluid is buoyed up by a force equal to the weight of the displaced fluid." (ONR, 1) A submarine therefore has to have the ability to regulate its buoyancy. Positive buoyancy places a submarine on the surface and with the use of ballast tanks, it then uses negative buoyancy. Flooding of the ballast tanks allows the submarine to slip beneath the waves to conduct its mission in the depths of the deep. Once submerged, the submarine must retain neutral buoyancy to avoid sinking to the bottom where, depending on the depth of the area could succumb to the external pressure and implode. Whether discussing an early Holland type submarine or the most recent United States Naval nuclear submarine, the process remains the same.

The origins of an undersea boat date back to the time of the ancients. An early mention of an undersea craft stems from the era of Alexander the Great, or so the legend goes.[11] As his forces were battling at Tyre, he ordered his "divers to destroy any submarine defenses the city might undertake to build." (CHINFO, 1) Though no records exist that he or any of his divers actually descended in a submersible, it is said that he did go into the depths in some sort of air holding craft.

Whether this fanciful tale is true or not, man's obsession with travel underwater has, over time, driven many inventors to speculate, build, and utilize technology to find a way to submerge underwater, remain there, explore, and ascend to the surface. The first major advancement in submarine design is attributed to William Bourne, a Royal Navy gunner who "designed a completely

---

[11] Leonardo Da Vinci also experimented with submarine technology. "He professed to have discovered the secret of remaining under water for a 'protracted period of time' but refused to reveal it to anybody. 'I do not publish or divulge [my method],' he declared, 'because of the evil nature of men who practice assassination at the bottom of the sea." (Parrish, 9)

enclosed boat that could be submerged and rowed beneath the surface."
(CHINFO, 1) Unfortunately, the idea never advanced to the building stage
however; his accomplishment in 1578 set the bar for further development.

In 1620, Cornelius Van Drebbel, a Dutch doctor built the world's first
practical submarine and tested it in the Thames River in England. Submerged
between 12 and 15 feet deep, the grease covered rowboat was powered by rowers
"pulling on oars that protruded through flexible leather seals in the hull."
(CHINFO, 2) Air was supplied by snorkel air tubes to the surface and it was able
to remain submerged for several hours.

Submarine technology in the early years was limited due to the lack of
any power source except those that were fueled by the power of man. Even with
that major disadvantage, designs proceeded, and in 1680, Giovanni Corelli
designed a version that included an attempt at the first "modern ballast tank."
(CHINFO, 2)   Each inventor provided their additions to the science of
submarines, but it was the influence of war that provided a major catalyst for
improvements.

In 1776, as war raged between the colonies and England, Yale graduate
David Bushnell attempted to attach a torpedo to the hull of the *H.M.S. Eagle* that
lie at anchor in New York Harbor. The *Turtle*, a one-man submarine, was six feet
long and was human powered by a crank which turned its propeller. The plan of
attack was as follows: submerge the *Turtle*, get close to the target, attach a
torpedo to the keel area and then pull away hopefully, all the while, avoiding
detection. The plan did not work out as he had expected. Though Bushnell had
wanted to pilot the craft himself, he had to allow an Army Sergeant, Ezra Lee,
the honors of the first documented attempt of an enemy attack by a submarine.
The attack was deemed a failure, as Lee was unable to attach the torpedo, but he
did manage to escape. In light of later submarine attacks, his attempt could be
considered a successful mission. (Harris, 6)

Replica of the *Turtle* at the U.S. Navy Submarine Museum. Author's collection.

The next inventor to try his hand at the submarine was Robert Fulton. Fulton had achieved success for his steam engine and provided a mechanical *Nautilus* for the French so that they could defeat the British fleet. Successfully tested in 1801, the *Nautilus* submerged to a depth of 25 feet and impressed the French nobility. The most significant additions to submarine design by Fulton were the classic cigar shape of the craft, a compressed air tank, and the periscope. Unfortunately, because it still utilized man power, the *Nautilus* lacked the killing punch necessary to be successful. (Harris, 9)

During the Danish Naval blockade of the German Port of Kiel, Wilhelm Bauer, a Prussian Army corporal built the *Brandtaucher* and it successfully moved the blockade further out to sea. In a subsequent run, the submarine faltered and sank into the mud at a depth of sixty feet. Amazingly, the three men escaped and survived. Again the submarine was powered by a two-man treadmill, trim was adjusted with a sliding weight, and buoyancy was controlled with ballast tanks.

Illustration of the *Alligator* submarine. Author's collection.

The War Between the States provided another proving ground for submarine development.[12] Most notably, the *H.L. Hunley* successfully sank the *U.S.S. Housatonic* off of Charleston, South Carolina. Unfortunately, the ill-fated craft, that had already taken two full crews – including one of her designers and

---

[12] Evidence exists indicating that over twenty sub-marine type craft were designed, tested, and utilized in varying degrees of effectiveness during the American Civil War. The most popular of the submarines were the *Hunley, Pioneer, Pioneer II* (aka *American Diver*), *Sub-Marine Explorer*, various *David* craft, and the *Intelligent Whale*. (Grohman)

namesake - to the bottom on previous tests, met a similar demise and upon retreat from the sinking Union vessel, sank to a watery grave.[13]

The first United States Navy submarine was also built and launched during the Civil War. The *Alligator*, a forty-six foot, sixteen man, man-powered submarine was placed into service in 1862, but as she was being towed into southern waters for use in the war effort, she filled with water and sank. Currently, a search is being conducted by the Office of Naval research, in an effort to locate this historical vessel.

During the Civil War years, other countries were also attempting to complete and master the use of submarine craft. In France, Charles Burn and Simon Bourgeois launched *Le Plongeur*, which was 140 feet long and had a 20 feet beam. It was powered by an engine that ran on compressed air. The concept and the vessel, however, proved to be unmanageable. (Harris, 16)

---

[13] It was found by Clive Cussler and members of NUMA in 1996 and was subsequently raised. The submarine is currently on view to the public in Charleston, South Carolina as it undergoes extensive restoration and preservation.

John P. Holland in the conning tower of the *Holland*. Courtesy U.S. Navy.

The next major player in the evolution of the submarine was John P. Holland. In 1878, his ideas already having been dismissed by the U.S. Navy, Holland received financial backing from the Fenian Brotherhood. He completed the *Holland* and was successful utilizing a gasoline engine. This prototype would eventually lead to the building of the *Fenian Ram*, which was a thirty-one foot long submarine, that worked well, but the time frame of completion frustrated the Brotherhood. The *Fenian Ram* and a smaller experimental submarine model were stolen by the Fenian Brotherhood in 1881.[14] Despite the setbacks, Holland continued to experiment and build submarine craft. After securing financial backing, he and several investors established the Nautilus Submarine Boat Company in 1883. Holland created and launched the *Zalinski* boat, but the submarine was not very successful and before it could be sold to the French government, the company went bankrupt. (Harris, 2-3)

In 1887, Holland and several other inventors and builders began competing for a coveted two million dollar contract for the United States Navy. (Harris, 5) Holland won the first competition, but due to several complications, the contract was withdrawn. A year later, Holland again won, but the monies were subsequently diverted to other naval appropriations. After several years of frustration and another round of open competition, Holland was awarded a two hundred thousand dollar contract to build the *Plunger*, an eighty five foot, steam powered submarine. (Harris, 5)

Though it worked, the *Plunger* did not work well. The steam powered engine caused the temperature of the submarine to reach an unbearable one hundred and thirty seven degrees. As worked progressed on the *Plunger*, Holland financed his next creation, simply named the *Holland VI*. The *Holland VI* was fifty-three feet long and gasoline powered. In May of 1897, the *Holland* was launched but the Spanish American War delayed further movement on behalf of the submarine by the United States Navy.[15]

At the same time, competing inventor and submarine builder, Simon Lake completed his *Argonaut*, a thirty-six foot submarine, complete with wheels for traveling along the bottom. It was delivered air through surface breathing

---

[14] The model was lost and the *Fenian Ram* was eventually retrieved. It is currently on display at a museum in Paterson, New Jersey.

[15] Following the Spanish-American War during a congressional hearing, Admiral Dewey commented on the possible effectiveness of submarine technology. "The senior officer noted that if the Spanish had had two submarines at Manila, he could not have captured and held the city. Besides he said, 'those crafts moving underwater would wear people out." (Harris, 10)

tubes. Lake however, would have to play second fiddle to Holland, as he would not receive a United States Navy contract for his designs until 1909.[16]

By 1900, the United States Navy purchased the *Holland VI* for one hundred and fifty thousand dollars. She was renamed the *U.S.S. Holland.* By August of the same year, six additional submarine boats of the *Holland* class were ordered for delivery and use by the United States Navy. Holland is credited as the father of the modern United States Navy Submarine Service, but looking back on the evolution of the submarine boat it was more a culmination of trials and errors by multiple designers and inventors that allowed for the eventual design and construction of a successful submarine. As submarines began to slip into the darkness of the abyss, a new type of warfare would emerge in their wake. After the sinking of the British ship *Falaba* in the Irish Sea and the later loss of the *Lusitania* both at the hands of German U-boats, the United States of America entered World War I.[17] Two World Wars and a Cold War later, the submarine, and its use in wartime, would be unparalleled.

A Holland submarine during trials. Author's collection.

---

[16] During this stagnant U.S. sales period, he sold his submarine, *Protector*, to the Russian Government in 1904. (Harris, 14)

[17] In June 1914, as the world marched toward the eventuality of a global conflict, "British Admiral Percy Scott wrote letters to the editors of the newspapers. In one he said 'as the motor has driven the horse from the road…so has the submarine driven the battleship from the sea." (Harris, 19)

President Roosevelt was a major supporter of the undersea torpedo boats. When he was the Assistant Secretary of the United States Navy, a post he was assigned to from 1897-1898, he had drafted a letter to his supervisor, Mr. John D. Long, Secretary of the Navy, explaining his views on the requisition of the submarine boats.

10 April, 1898

My Dear Mr. Secretary:

I think the Holland submarine boat should be purchased. Evidently she has great possibilities in her for harbor defense. Sometime she doesn't work perfectly, but often she does, and I don't think in the present emergency we can afford to let her slip. I recommend that you authorize the Bureau of Construction to do so, which would be just as well.

Very sincerely yours,

T. Roosevelt

But the letter did not expedite the process of the purchase of the Holland submarine, as it was not purchased by the United States Navy until April 18, 1900. Commissioned later that year on October 12, 1900, the *U.S.S. Holland* entered service after many modifications, tests, retests and changes had been put into place. Submarines of the *Adder* class, including the *Plunger, Adder, Grampus, Moccasin, Pike, Porpoise,* and *Shark,* would be delivered to the United States Navy starting during Roosevelt's presidency in 1901.

But the submarines were initially frowned upon by the United States Navy's officers and duty on board was probably thought as a punishment by some of the upper echelon officers. The pig boats as they were sometimes referred as, did not offer much of a future for the junior officers that were assigned to command them.[18] The apparent lack of vision by the United States Navy brass would not affect President Roosevelt's enthusiasm for the invention as he ordered the *U.S.S. Plunger* to Oyster Bay for review. Despite the overwhelming lack of support from the top levels of naval leadership, to Roosevelt the submarine marked, like her larger dreadnaught sisters of his envisioned fleet, a vital aspect to an effective and efficient naval force.

---

[18] Attitudes changed, thanks in large part to both Roosevelt and the technological advances in submarine design and efficiency. A young Lieutenant named Chester Nimitz took command of the *U.S.S. Plunger* and two other submarines during this era. "Thanks in large part to the efforts [of Nimitz]…the obnoxious and dangerous gasoline engine was replaced by diesels, beginning with Nimitz's fourth submarine command *Skipjack*. (circa 1911) (Harris, 18) A year later, Lt. Nimitz addressed the Naval War College in Rhode Island regarding "Defensive and Offensive Tactics of Submarines." (Harris, 18) Nimitz would end his career as one of the most celebrated naval officers of his time.

Chapter 5 - A Naval Historian

Though not his first publication, *The Naval War of 1812 or The History of the United States Navy during the last war with Great Britain*, published in 1882 was Roosevelt's first seminal work that brought him recognition as an historian. According to John Allen Gable the book "immediately established the author as a notable historian, and the book has endured generation after generation, as a classic in the canon of American Naval history." (Gable, ix) *The Naval War of 1812* would become a staple volume aboard every commissioned United States naval vessel upon its publication and once its message splashed into both public and military-circles.[19]

Roosevelt was already researching and writing *The Naval War of 1812 or The History of the United States Navy during the last war with Great Britain* while a senior at Harvard. He did not take any time to finish the manuscript, but rather he "went hunting in the Midwest," entered "law school at Columbia University in the fall" and married Alice Hathaway Lee. (Gable, ix) After his first year of law school, he and his bride toured Europe; he climbed the Matterhorn, was nominated for the New York State Assembly, was elected to that post, and finished the manuscript of his research.[20]

---

[19] According to "regulations adopted in 1886, at least one copy of *The Naval War of 1812* was to be placed on board every vessel in the U.S. Navy." (Gable, xiii)

[20] As pointed out by John Gable in his introduction for The Modern Library edition of *The Naval War of 1812*, Roosevelt had thoroughly engrossed himself in his research for the book. His friend Owen Wister, stated "...He finished his *Naval History of the War of 1812* mostly standing on one leg at the bookcases in his New York house, the other leg crossed behind, toe touching the floor, heedless of dinner engagements and the flight of time. A slide drew out from the bookcase. On this he had open the leading authorities on navigation, of which he knew nothing. He knew that when a ship's course was one way, with the wind another, the ship had to sail at angles, and this was called tacking or beating. By exhaustive study and drawing of models, he pertinaciously got it all right, whatever of it came into the naval engagements he was writing about. His wife used to look in at his oblivious back, and exclaim in a plaintive drawl: 'We're dining out in Twenty minutes, and Teedy's drawing little ships!" (Gable, xii)

When one thinks about the accomplishments during this period in his life, it must be tempered with the overall breadth of work and accomplishments that Roosevelt completed during his overall life as an author, politician, etc. But what influenced Roosevelt to write a thorough history of a naval war? A family-naval influence was the answer. Two of Roosevelt's uncles, James Dunwody Bulloch and Irvine Bulloch had both been naval officers. James Bulloch was a United States Navy officer who "became an admiral in the Confederate navy during the Civil War." (Gable, x) The younger uncle, Irvine Bulloch was also a naval officer and had served on the *C.S.S. Alabama*.[21] Following the end of the hostilities, both of Roosevelt's uncles had remained in England in exile. But the connection remained and "TR and his family, in spite of distance, maintained close ties with the Bullochs in England," and visited them on trips to Europe. (Gable, x) Roosevelt "told his friend Reverend Ferdinand Cowel Inglehart, a Methodist Minister, in the 1890's:

> *From my earliest recollections I have been fed on tales of the sea and of ships. My mother's brother was an admiral in the Confederate navy, and her deep interest in the Southern course and her brother's calling led her to talk to me as a little shaver about ships, ships, ships, and fighting of ships, till they sank into the depths of my soul. And when I first began to think, in any independent order,...I began to write a history of the Naval War of 1812." (Gable, x)*

Though he had grown up surrounded by a fleet of stories, yarns and tales of the sea, Roosevelt had to become a student of the navy, and more importantly, its strategy. Roosevelt devoured all available information and read the works of

---

[21] The *C.S.S. Alabama* was one of the "most famous of the Confederate commerce raiders" having "captured sixty-four ships in her career." (Anderson, 209, 207) The *C.S.S. Alabama*, after coaling in Cherbourg, France, engaged the *U.S.S. Kearsarge*. "The ships steamed in a circle with the range gradually dropping to about 400 yards," but the reinforced hull of the *U.S.S. Kearsarge*, coupled with a defective Confederate shell that had failed to explode in her rudder, was the victor. (Anderson, 208) The feared Confederate raider– the *C.S.S. Alabama* – succumbed to the battle and sank to the bottom.

William James, James Fenimore Cooper, Admiral Jurien de la Grauiere, and Admiral George Emmons. In addition to books related to the War of 1812, he also collected and studied primary sources of information from both sides of the Atlantic, spoke with various professors, naval tacticians, and of course, his uncle James Bulloch. A visit with Uncle James solidified Roosevelt's work and fueled James' own work, *The Secret Service of the Confederate States in Europe*, which was published in 1883. But most importantly he "began mastering the tactics, technology, and terminology of naval warfare." (Gable, xi) Roosevelt, though he had spent time sailing small boats from his home from Long Island, he had known little of the necessities of sailing and especially of sailing into battle.[22]

Well received "on both sides of the Atlantic," *The Naval War of 1812 or The History of the United States Navy during the last war with Great Britain* would become an instant classic, going through two printings in 1882. In 1883, Roosevelt added additional text including a "long preface, in which he summarized the land operations during the war, and a new concluding chapter on the Battle of New Orleans." (Gable, xii) As he attempted, Roosevelt had produced a fair and balanced view of the conflict. As pointed out by Gable in his introduction, Roosevelt was asked to write an account of the naval war for the official history of the Royal Navy, which was also reprinted in the United States as *The Naval Operations of the War Between Great Britain and the United States, 1812-1815.*

The book provided the foundation for Roosevelt not only as a historian but also as a distinguished naval strategist. The *New York Times* review of the book, which was published on June 5, 1882, summarized Roosevelt's work:

> *"The volume is an excellent one in every respect, and shows in so young an author the best promise for a good historian – fearlessness of stated, caution, endeavor to be impartial, an a brisk and interesting way of telling events. It may be thoroughly recommended to take the*

---

[22] Roosevelt, with the exception of small rowboats, etc., would never own a boat.

And take the place of other volumes - most of which, as Roosevelt has pointed out in his introductory pages, were impartial and inaccurate – it did. As a result of his profound naval research and his sudden rise to scholarship within the naval circles, he was asked to speak at the Naval War College on various occasions. These speeches, which would continue into his days as President, also led to a friendship with Captain Alfred Thayer Mahan, an accomplished naval strategist as well.[23]

Original copies of Thayer's and Roosevelt's research at the Sagamore Hill National Park. Author's collection.

---

[23] Though Mahan's book, *The Influence of Sea Power upon History 1660-1783* is highly regarded as a classic in naval affairs, it was Roosevelt that largely spurred his research. When Roosevelt's work, *The Naval War of 1812* was published, Mahan was an "obscure, forty-year-old career officer of no particular accomplishment, writing or otherwise." The two men however would champion one another for the remainder of their lives. (Morris, 599) Author Richard West Jr. in *Admirals of American Empire*, paints a rather poor portrait of Roosevelt in relation to Mahan. Though Richards indicates several times that Mahan was the mentor to Roosevelt, it was ultimately Roosevelt that put Mahan's theories to practical use. "When in April of 1897 Theodore Roosevelt worked his way into the Navy Department as Assistant Secretary, Captain Mahan had not only a nationwide audience for his writings but a vigorous forthright executive within the Department who as a long time friend and pupil was completely sold on Mahan's doctrine and determined, come hell or high water, to put Mahan's program into effect." (Richard, 161)

The last legacy of the book identified that the United States had to make, "military preparedness, particularly naval power, an integral part of American nationalism." (Gable, xiv) In 1897, Roosevelt was appointed to the position of Assistant Secretary of the Navy. It would be an opportunity to test his theories and assertion in the real waters of naval preparedness and more importantly, battle.

Chapter 6 - Assistant Secretary of the Navy

Roosevelt had been an integral part of the election campaign for President McKinley and there were some including Henry Cabot Lodge that wanted Theodore Roosevelt to be provided a position within the government. But McKinley and others were afraid that Roosevelt might have plans that went against the overall administration's policy of peace. The political pressure continued and McKinley was hesitant to offer the position to someone who voiced his concerns, thoughts, and plans, so openly, like Roosevelt. In one correspondence written to Lodge when it seemed apparent that he was not to be chosen, Roosevelt stated "I should have been entirely loyal and subordinate." (Pringle, 117) Pringle continues to explain that when there was once again a glimmer of hope that he might be appointed to the position, Roosevelt again corresponded with Lodge in regards to his would be supervisor, Secretary of the Navy, John D. Long, saying that "I want him to understand that I shall stay at Washington, hot weather or any other weather, whenever he wants me to stay there, and go wherever he sends me, and my aim should be solely to make his administration as success." (Pringle, 117)

President McKinley appointed Roosevelt to the position and Congress, after only three days, confirmed the appointment. Though Roosevelt would only hold the position for a relatively short period of time, he made the most of his time within the post.[24] Though the administration had pushed for peace with the Spanish, Roosevelt was a proponent of going to war to test the machine of both the Navy and the Army. But the Spanish were not the only issue in which Roosevelt raised concern. He also was outspoken in other naval matters including

---

[24] According to a speech given by Edward J. Renehan Jr. on October 29, 1999, four other Roosevelt men, including Franklin, Theodore Jr., Theodore Douglas (Corinne Roosevelt's son), Henry Latrobe, would serve in the capacity of Assistant Secretary of the Navy. (Theodore Roosevelt Association website)

the construction of a canal to link the Atlantic and Pacific Oceans and for the annexation of the Hawaiian Islands.[25]

Assistant Secretary of the Navy Roosevelt in his office. Author's collection.

The Secretary of the Navy was John D. Long. His attitudes were more in line with McKinley's and he was less of a catalyst for change. With Long in charge of the United States Navy, there was hope that Roosevelt's actions would be tempered by his superior. Roosevelt had loudly voiced his opinion so it was to no surprise that McKinley had his doubts. According to Pringle, Roosevelt in October of 1894 was "demanding the annexation of the Hawaiian Islands and the construction of an oceanic canal through Nicaragua." (Pringle, 116) In addition, he also stated to the "National Republican Club on May 28, 1895, that he favored the establishment of a navy that will sustain the honor of the American Flag. I want to see the Monroe Doctrine upheld in its entirety. I believe in these policies with all my heart and soul." Would Roosevelt's passion and fervor be dampened by the cautious and conservative Long or would his thought regarding naval

---

[25] According to author Richard West, "With Theodore Roosevelt, as with Mahan, the annexation of Hawaii amounted to a passion." (West, 305)

supremacy turn to the action as he stood on the proverbial bridge of the United States Navy?

Roosevelt, soon after his appointment had opportunities at the helm. In April of 1897, the Japanese were "looking at the Hawaiian Islands with covetous eyes." (Pringle, 119) On the 22nd, as Long was absent from his duties, Roosevelt in command "assured President McKinley that the *U.S.S. Philadelphia* was already at Hawaii and that other vessels could steam there swiftly." (Pringle, 119) Secretary Long was not as keen on a possible build up of the fleet in the Pacific. Though Roosevelt had had kept his feelings beneath the sonar of the public on most accounts, he had written to his friend A.T. Mahan regarding his ideals. In those written exchanges, Roosevelt clearly declared that the country should "build a dozen new battleships, half of them on the Pacific Coast... I am fully alive to the danger of Japan." (Pringle, 120)

During May of 1897, Roosevelt spent time in New York at the New York Navy Yard, to conduct an investigation into alleged inappropriate actions by "various department heads." Workmen at the yard had stated that special treatment was being provided to two engineers' friends from out of town, instead of local laborers. The investigation, which was concluded shortly after, did not pull Roosevelt away from his continued pursuit of other plans and he continued to correspond with Mahan as he prepared for his upcoming remarks at the Naval War College.

On June 2, 1897, Roosevelt made an address at the Naval War College in Newport, Rhode Island.[26] His short-lived tenure of keeping his thoughts relegated to the internal circles of the fleet and government were once again out in the open.[27] He once again publicly decried peace and issued a plea for a strong

---

[26] According to Edmund Morris, the speech "turned out to be the first greatest speech of his career, a fanfare call to arms which echoed all the more resounding for the pause that had preceded it." (Morris, 593)

[27] Roosevelt spent many hours at the Metropolitan club in Washington, D.C. during this time frame. He utilized the time to align with those who also expressed expansionist thoughts and ideals. The crowd normally "consisted of Senators and Representatives,

naval fleet. On July 30, 1897, Roosevelt witnessed a review of the New York and Brooklyn battalions of the Naval Militia" held at the grounds of Fort Hamilton in New York. The men had completed a series of tests and maneuvers over the course of several days aboard the steamships *Massachusetts* and *Texas*. During his remarks to the sailors, Roosevelt stated that he was "pleased, because he knew he could count upon on their working and not playing sailors, and considers them as an element always immediately available for the active, rough work of fighting." (*NYT*, 31JUL1897) "One or two more belligerent speeches were made during the Summer of 1897 and these so distressed Navy Secretary Long that Roosevelt, again, promised to reform." (Pringle, 121) Though Roosevelt argued that all he was doing was advocating for additional ships, the Secretary must have felt hesitantly confident in leaving Roosevelt in command of the Navy, even for short periods of time. In the late summer of 1897 with the temperature rising not only in the humid capital of the United States, but also in the steamy tropics of Cuba, Secretary Long took a short absence from his duties as Secretary. Roosevelt was once again at the helm – the United States Navy at his beck and call.[28]

Over the next few months, it was "not easy to draw a line between Roosevelt's anxiety to build up the navy, which was legitimate preparedness, and his lust for war." (Pringle, 112) Roosevelt utilized other duties as Assistant

---

Navy and Army officers, writers, socialites, lawyers, and scientists - men liked as much by Roosevelt's motley personality as by their common political belief, namely, that Manifest Destiny called for the United States to free Cuba, annex Hawaii, and raise the American flag supreme over the Western Hemisphere." He also befriended many naval officers, including Commodore George Dewey, as he conducted his business within the Navy Department. (Morris, 592)

[28] During this time frame, Roosevelt authored an anthology that was printed by the Government Printing Office. Though Secretary Long required Roosevelt to include "in my opinion" (referring to Roosevelt) "somewhere in the Introduction to show that it was not an official statement of policy by the Navy Department," the short volume was approved. McKinley, who also was provided an advanced version of the volume titled *The Naval Policy of Americas Outlined in Messages of the Presidents of the United States from the Beginning to the Present Day*, also authorized and approved of Roosevelt's work and publication. (Morris, 608)

Secretary of the Navy to gain elicit support and advocate for the importance of the United States Navy.[29] On the one hundredth anniversary of the launching of the *U.S.S. Constitution* on October 21, 1897, Roosevelt was one of many dignitaries on hand in Boston, Massachusetts. During his remarks, he stated that "the moment of the Constitution's launching was the beginning of our navy as we know it today. It was fifteen years after the launching of the *Constitution* and her sister ships before that proud flag which menaced us was humbled, and during that fifteen years there were many people who objected to the maintenance of the navy." (*NYT*, 22OCT1897) Roosevelt also submitted an exhaustive report regarding the "personnel of the navy." (*NYT*, 31DEC1897) Roosevelt had been "charged by a special board to consider the report upon means to breakup the...stagnation in promotions...to settle the long standing differences between the line and Engineer Corps....and to devise a betterment of the conditions of enlisted men aboard ship." (*NYT*, 31DEC1897)

Roosevelt felt that the recommendations were "absolutely essential" to support the United States Navy. Roosevelt stated "that the best naval officer of the future shall be proficient in engineering." (*NYT*, 31DEC1897) He continued:

> *"The fact that Farragut knew nothing of engines has no more bearing on the case than the fact that Blake knew nothing of sails. Exactly as Nelson, who succeeded Blake, had to know details of naval matters of which Blake was ignorant, so the Farragut of the future must know what the great victor of New Orleans and Mobile Bay had no chance to learn. This is an age of specialization; but there can be no specialization in command. In time it may very possibly prove desirable to differentiate, less by law than by departmental custom, among officers at sea, so as to employ each principally along the lines for which he shows the most*

---

[29] Roosevelt also continued to advocate for Mahan's work. Roosevelt's rave review of Mahan's book, *The Influence of Sea Power upon History 1660-1783*, resulted in *The Atlantic Monthly* asking Mahan to write an article on naval policy. The article - The United States Looking Outward – "was the stuff and marrow of imperialistic doctrine flung to a wide audience beyond the elite circle of Tracy, Roosevelt and Lodge." (West, 148)

aptitude, but they must remain line officers, the major part of whose duties are identical, and the engineer must differ from his fellows only in the same manner as the navigator or the ordnance expert does."

Roosevelt then further addressed the problems with line and engineer corps differences:

"The problem of combining the line and the engineers is comparatively new. The system of promotion by pure seniority is admirably calculated to produce long stagnation in the lower ranks, to secure the attainment of command only after the age when a man should begin to exercise command has passed, and finally to make the promotion of an officer dependent not upon the zealous performance of his duties, but upon the possession of a good stomach, and of an easy nature; while a positive premium is put upon the man who never ventures to take a risk, and who therefore never does anything great, but who also, of course, avoids the chance of what would seem failure in the eyes of the less venturesome. But the simple process of consulting any set of actuary tables, it can be seen at a glance that the system insures a man spending much the largest part of his life, including his most active and vigorous years, in a subordinate capacity, including normally a quarter of a century, as a lieutenant, while at the very end, when long service in subordinate positions has dulled his energy, and probably rendered him unfitted to bear responsibilities, he is thrust for a brief period into a command rank, and is galloped at absurd speed through the grades of commander, captain, commodore, and admiral."

In conclusion, Roosevelt reiterated the importance of Congress reviewing the organization plan:

The bill is so obviously in the interest of the whole service, it will so unquestionably benefit that service and raise the profession of the United States naval officer to a still higher level, that it seems unlike that there will be serious objection to what it proposes to do, save perhaps on one point. This is the matter of expense. If the recommendations of the board are carried out there will *be an additional cost of nearly $600,000. I not only recommend it in the is case, but I wish to state with all the emphasis possible that in my judgment of the question of expense is unimportant with the benefit to be gained." (NYT 31DEC1897)*

As the reorganization bill went forth to be reviewed, Roosevelt continued writing Secretary Long regarding his other recommendations.[30] In a series of letters, Roosevelt recommended to Long that they should take "firm action on behalf of the wretched Cubans," suggesting sending the fleet to Cuba and a "flying squadron against Spain itself." (Pringle, 122) He also pleaded to have the "Asiatic Squadron steam for the Philippines as soon as war had been declared." (Pringle, 112) But the memorandums fell on deaf ears. On February 15, 1898, all of that would change with a deafening and deadly explosion in the serene waters of Havana.

The *U.S.S. Maine* was on station in Havana Harbor when it mysteriously exploded. The ship sank quickly taking with her two officers and two hundred and sixty-four sailors. Telegrams and news reports spoke of the tragedy – some stating it was an accident, others stating that the incident was an act of war. The American public was outraged at the destruction of the ship and loss of their sailors. Though no answer was provided by the captain of the sunken battleship, Capt. Sigsbee had asked everyone, including the public, to hold out in their opinion until an investigation into the cause of the incident could be determined. But the rage of the American public, fueled by newspaper editors such as Hearst and others, sent the majority of Americans on the quest for revenge. Soon the call of the public was to "Remember the *Maine*."

---

[30] An editorial in the March 17, 1898 issue of the *New York Times* addressed what had become known as the Roosevelt bill. "For some dozen years we have been more or less engaged in securing the material for a navy – the ships and armament. For that purpose we have spent much money and have achieved results with which we may be more than content. But for the use of ships and armament such as war requires the human machinery is just as necessary as the other, and much more difficult to obtain expect by the firm and intelligent application of an adequate and consistent system." (*NYT*, 17MAR1898)

On February 25, 1898, amidst the crisis, Secretary Long took the afternoon off. It would be a fateful act as Roosevelt took the opportunity to send Admiral George Dewey a cable:

"Keep full of coal. In event of declaration of war Spain, your duty will be to see that the Spanish Squadron does not leave the Asiatic coast, and then offensive operations in the Philippine Islands." (Potter, 122)

Assistant Secretary of the Navy Roosevelt. Circa 1897. National Archives.

Long, in his diary wrote that the decision to leave Roosevelt in charge for the afternoon was as if "the very devil had seemed to possess" Roosevelt. (Pringle, 124) "Like a bull in a china shop," Long continued regarding how Roosevelt had acted during his absentia from the helm. As Pringle points out and as others agree, the cable sent to Dewey under Roosevelt's command however, "made possible the naval victory at Manila Bay."[31] (Pringle, 125) Long, though admittedly upset at Roosevelt would, years later, look back on his working with Roosevelt with a fonder outlook. When his two volume history, *The New American Navy* was published in December of 1903, he stated the following about Roosevelt:

> *"His ardor sometimes went faster than the President or the department approved. Just before the war, when the Spanish battle fleet was on its way here, he as well as some naval officers, regarding that as a cause of war, approved of sending a squadron to meet it without waiting for a more formal declaration of war. He worked indefatigably, frequently incorporating his views in memoranda which he would place every morning on my desk. Most of his suggestions, had, however, so far as applicable, been already adapted by the various bureaus, the Chiefs of which were straining every nerve and leaving nothing not done. When I suggested to him that some future historians reading his memoranda, if they were put on record, would get the impression that the bureaus were inefficient, he accepted the suggestion with the generous good nature which is so marked in him. Indeed, noting could be pleasanter than our relations. His typewriter had no rest. He, like most of us, lacks the rare knack of brevity. He was especially stimulating to the younger officers who gathered about him and made his office as busy as a hive."[32] (NYT, 12DEC1903)*

---

[31] Roosevelt was instrumental in getting Dewey control of the fleet. During Richard West's explanation of how Dewey came to command the Asiatic Squadron, he portrays Roosevelt's recollection of events poorly. "Long, a conscientious politician from Massachusetts, was kept in such a perpetual state of trepidation by the vigorous, red-blooded warmongering of his Assistant Secretary that his reliability as a historian suffers. Roosevelt, the fire-eating imperialist, fearful lest America lose her place in the sun through plutocratic, fatty degeneration of the warlike spirit, was a Procrustean historian and a notorious distorter of fact." (West, 143) Whether Roosevelt's recollection of how Dewey came to command the fleet, the fact that Dewey was at the helm, assured victory when war finally came to the Philippines.

[32] Interestingly on February 3, 1904 a dispatch from Washington that was received in Boston indicated that Long's book would "not be purchased by the Navy Department Bureau for use on board the United States naval vessels, probably because of its implied criticisms of President Roosevelt when the latter was Assistant Secretary of the Navy." (*NYT*, 4FEB1904) Long, who was questioned by a reporter over the dispatch stated

On March 28, 1898 Congress received the report on the *U.S.S. Maine* explosion indicating that the *"Maine* had been destroyed by a submarine mine." War was inevitable in light of the news and the already mounting public sentiment toward aggression, even though President McKinley and the Spanish government still pursued peace. The nation however would not allow a peaceful summation of the incident. Roosevelt had finally gotten his war, but interestingly, his post as the Assistant Secretary of the Navy, was not a close enough seat for him during the march to war.[33] Instead he resigned his position and offered his services and leadership to a cavalry regiment.[34]

On May 6th Roosevelt sat at his desk, which had previously been used by Assistant Secretary of the Navy, Gustavus Fox, and drafted a letter to his superiors, Secretary of the Navy and the President.[35] In his letter of resignation, Roosevelt thanked Secretary Long for his "resolute disinteredness and single-minded devotion to the public interest." (*NYT*, 12MAY1898) Roosevelt concluded his letter by stating that he had "grown not merely to respect you [Long] as my superior officer, but to value your friendship very highly…permit me to sign myself, with great affection and respect." (*NYT*, 12MAY1898) The following day Long replied to the letter and stated that "as I have told you so many times I have it [the letter of resignation] with the utmost regret. I have often

commented that he was 'apparently not much concerned over the statement." (*NYT*, 4FEB1904)

[33] Admiral Mahan, who had been appointed to the Naval War Board, stayed in Roosevelt's Washington home, in his absence, "for the duration of the war." (West, 214)

[34] On April 30, 1898 – the same day that the American Squadron under command of Admiral Dewey was off the entrance to Manila Bay - Roosevelt sent a letter, on official Navy Department letterhead, to Brooks Brothers in New York City. "Can you make me so I shall have it here by next Saturday a blue cravennat [sp] regular lieutenant-colonel's uniform without yellow on collar and with leggings? If so make it. (Signed) Theodore Roosevelt."

[35] The desk, which Roosevelt had brought up from the basement of the Navy Department, was a "massive piece of mahogany used by Assistant Secretary Gustavus Fox, another juvenile hero, during the Civil War." The desk was adorned with "two beautifully carved monitors which bulged out of each side-panel trailing rudders and anchors, and a group of wooden cannons protecting the wooden stars and stripes." (Morris, 590)

expressed perhaps too emphatically and harshly, my conviction that you ought not to leave the post of Assistant Secretary of the Navy, where your services have not only been of such great value, but of so much inspiration to me and to the whole service." (*NYT*, 12MAY1898) Long continued, "your energy, industry, and great knowledge of naval interests, and especially your inspiring influence in stimulating and lifting the whole tone of personnel of the navy, have been invaluable." (*NYT*, 12MAY1898) In closing, Long wished him luck at the front. On May 9th, Secretary of the President, John Addison Porter replied to Roosevelt's May 6, 1898 letter of resignation. In addition to commenting on the President's regret over Roosevelt's leaving, Porter confirmed to Roosevelt that his "services here during your entire term of office have been faithful, able, and successful in the highest degree, and no one appreciates this fact more keenly than the President…without doubt, your connection with the navy will be beneficially felt in several of its departments for many years to come." (*NYT*, 12MAY1898) Roosevelt left the Department of the Navy bound for a horse and saddle on May 10, 1898.[36] His involvement in the affairs of the United States Navy would remain in port, for the majority of the duration of the war, but would soon return to sea, as Roosevelt was elected to public office. As Governor-Elect, Roosevelt published his first article in *The North American Review*, regarding the importance of reorganization of the personnel in the Navy. Roosevelt, as per the *New York Times* advanced review of the article, explained the need for more than just ships but also the right men to man them in battle. Having completed his

---

[36] Roosevelt's departure from the Naval Department on May 10, 1898 was attended by many of his colleagues and associates. "It is safe to say that not one of the employes [sp] from the highest to the lowest, declined the invitation," to the Assistant Secretary's last day. "There were many expressions of regret at his departure, and the whole affair was lacking in that perfunctory character which is often attaches to ceremonies of the kind." (*NYT*, 11MAY 1898) Several employees presented Mr. Roosevelt "a very handsome silver-mounted cavalry sabre which he [Roosevelt] displayed with pride upon his desk to all of his callers." (*NYT*, 11MAY1898)

tour of duty and having gained a first–hand experience in battle, he was well aware of the human aspect of warfare, both on land and at sea.[37]

> *"It is useless to spend millions of dollars in the building of perfect fighting machines, unless we make the personnel which is to handle these machines equally perfect. We have an excellent navy now; but we can never afford to relax our efforts to make it better still. Next time we may have to face some enemy far more formidable than Spain. In my judgment, the personnel bill will markedly increase the efficiency of our already efficient officers." (NYT, 1DEC1898)*

Roosevelt, his time as Assistant Secretary of the Navy albeit short, illustrated his building of his naval knowledge, his understanding of the politics of naval circles with governmental torpedo boats lurking on the horizon, and the importance of continued building of ships and the training of the men charged with steaming them into battle. Pringle, in his biography of Roosevelt summed up Roosevelt's brief tenure as the Assistant Secretary of the Navy in one sentence -"Roosevelt might have lived up to his pledges of good conduct, made in all sincerity, had he served in less exciting times."

---

[37] Roosevelt's heroics during the Spanish-American War made him a national hero. Roosevelt's association with the Rough Riders would be an important stage for his eventual rise to the Presidency of the United States.

Chapter 7 - Beneath the Waves

President Roosevelt drafted a letter during the morning hours of Saturday August 25, 1905 to his son, Kermit Roosevelt. In the letter the President explained his delight of having received his son's note and that since Kermit left that "life has gone on just as usual here," referring to Sagamore Hill. (Irwin, 108) After providing insight to his father's and families' activities, he states that "The Plunger has come to the Bay and I am going out on it this afternoon-or rather down on it." The letter continues later that day with the conclusion, "N.B. I have just been, for 50 minutes; it was very interesting." (Irwin, 108)

U.S.S. Plunger **out of the water for repairs. Courtesy U.S. Navy.**

So the President, after stating that he was not going to go on, and certainly not under the waves onboard the *U.S.S. Plunger*, did just that. The brevity of the note to Kermit was not a direct reflection on the profound experience of his undersea trip onboard the *U.S.S. Plunger*. The *New York Times* ran the story on page one of their August 26, 1905 issue with the article titled,

"President Takes Plunge in Submarine." The subheadings provided additional highlights including, "Remains Below the Surface for Fifty-five Minutes, ONCE 40 FEET UNDER WATER, He Manoeuvres the Vessel Himself and is Greatly Pleased – Divers Were at Hand."[38]

So "despite official denials that he intended to risk lie in a submarine, President Roosevelt shortly after 3 o'clock this afternoon went aboard the Holland type submarine boat." The originally planned exhibition with his wife and guests from the relative safety of the *Sylph* had been postponed due to the inclement weather conditions as "sheets of rain were falling when the President left Sagamore Hill in the afternoon in an automobile." He drove down to the pier where the surf was crashing over the wooden slats of the pier. A stiff and relentless northeasterly wind howled sending sea spray all around. Clad in a khaki shirt and pants, the President put on a set of oilskins to assist in keeping himself somewhat dry for his trip to the submarine. At the pier, the motor launch *Dart* awaited his arrival.

After Roosevelt boarded the *Dart*, the launch cast of its lines and headed for the U.S. Navy tugboat *Apache* that was acting as submarine tender for the trip to Oyster Bay. After the transit, the motor launch pulled alongside the *Apache* while the submarine awaited the President's arrival abeam of the launch. "Roosevelt boarded the *Apache*, crossed her decks, and stepped into the conning tower of the underwater craft where he was received by Lieut. Charles Preston Nelson." Roosevelt's underwater adventure where he would be the first President to go underwater by the means of a submersible craft was about to begin.

As the wind blew and the sheets of rain continued to call, the *U.S.S. Plunger* cast off its tending lines and was finally free to begin her trails. As the submarine began to make headway out to the Long Island Sound, the *Apache*

---

[38] The amount of time Roosevelt spent onboard the submarine varies depending on the source referenced. According to the deck logs of the *U.S.S.T.B. Plunger*, filled out and signed by Lt. Nelson, Roosevelt boarded the submarine at 3:30 P.M. and departed at 6:10 P.M. A complete transcription of the deck logs for this time period is included in Appendix A.

followed in her wake, but once the submarine had reached two miles off shore, "the order was passed to the *Apache* to stand by."

The submarine then sank below the surface of the Long Island Sound. Only the conning tower was still visible for a few moments. Then she sank deeper below the surface, her periscope keeping the only vigil with the above surface world. The submarine stabilized at twenty or so feet and remained stationary and "Roosevelt was shown the various parts of the mechanism."

The President showed special "interest in the torpedo mechanism, and throughout the tour of inspection behaved like a delighted schoolboy over everything he saw." During this part of the inspection, Roosevelt spoke with the commander of the vessel and various members of the crew, complimenting them on the "efficiency of their management."

During the tour, he inspected and interviewed T.P. Ryan, who was in charge of the very necessary and vital aspect of air supply, the gunnery crew, as well as the machinist mates. After he had toured the submarine's compartments, he "accompanied Lieut. Nelson to the conning tower, from which he viewed the experiments."

While in the conning tower, Roosevelt was shown how the periscope, or the "telescopic contrivance which brings the surface view within the sight of those below," and how it worked. At this point, his tour of the various compartments inspected, the submarine was engaged in forward propulsion. After making headway forward, the submarine came to neutral and then proceeded backward in an attempt to show the maneuverability of the craft. All the while, Roosevelt watched enthusiastically as the various gears and levers were calibrated to engage movement. Once he was familiar with the gadgetry, "he himself maneuvered the vessel until he was thoroughly acquainted with the signals and levers."

After the President steered the craft, the submarine descended to the bottom, "a distance of forty feet below the surface." The *Apache* stood its vigil nearby and as the *U.S.S. Plunger* rested towards the bottom of the murky depths of the Long Island Sound, a school of porpoise swam by which "interested the President, who watched their movements for some time," from the portholes of the submarine's conning tower.

With Lieutenant Nelson at the helm, the *U.S.S. Plunger* went through a series of drills while underway and below the surface. Nelson sent the submarine boat forward and backward, up and down bow first then stern first, the submarine breaking the surface intermittently as the *Apache* rolled in the distance. After those drills had been accomplished, Nelson leveled the boat out at twenty feet below the surface and began a demonstration to illustrate the speed and maneuverability of the undersea craft. He sped forward to full speed and then signaled for reverse to return to the original location. The President "expressed his delight at the speed with which the maneuver was accomplished."

The last test of the maneuverability of the submarine was accomplished when Nelson sped forward, came to a complete stop, then reversed to remain perfectly still in the water. This experiment "seemed especially interesting to the President in view of its value in time of war with the supposition that the *Plunger* should be opposed by other submarine boats."

But "one of the most thrilling experiments" was about to begin while onboard the *U.S.S. Plunger* as all of the lights were turned off in an experiment that was a continuation of the previous maneuver. "Carried out in the gloom of the Sound bottom with a clarity and accuracy" the President stated that he had "never seen anything so remarkable."

Soon the "black of the water turned to gray, then to green, followed by an opal tint: then the white light of day shone through the portholes," as the submarine ascended to the surface. The hatch of the conning tower was opened and the stale air of the running submarine was replaced by fresh humid air from the outside. The total time under the water was a little under one hour.

The President thanked Lieutenant Nelson and the crew of the *U.S.S. Plunger* for his trip below the surface and explained that he was "very much impressed with the submarine boat." The submarine returned to the *Apache* and soon the President bid farewell to the submarine and her crew and was back onboard the *Apache* where he then transferred back to the *Dart*. The President then motored back to the pier returned to the safe confines of Sagamore Hill and described his trip.

Now that the trip had taken place, the public could learn of the President's perceived dangerous adventure below the waves in the new creation. But according to the article, the precautions "taken to prevent the knowledge of the President's trip in the *U.S.S. Plunger* becoming public" were less extensive then the precautions taken prior to the *U.S.S. Plunger*'s arrival at Oyster Bay.

In addition to the eyebolts that had been added to the submarine to be used in the unlikely event of the submarine sinking to the bottom, the overhaul of the electronic equipment, "a diver was also on board while others accompanied the *Plunger* aboard the tender *Apache*." Though President Roosevelt had eluded his secret service agents and quite possibly his own wife to take the trip, the *New York Times* reported that the following day the *U.S.S. Plunger* would again provide an exhibition for Mrs. Roosevelt and some guests from the deck of the *Sylph*.

Roosevelt was later reported as having said as he climbed out of the hatch of the *U.S.S. Plunger* that "I've had many a splendid day's fun in my life, but I can't remember ever having crowded so much of it into such a few hours." (Hagedorn, 228) The experience was both eventful for the President and the men of the submarine service. Three days later on August 28, 1905, Roosevelt wrote a letter to Charles Joseph Bonaparte, the Secretary of the Navy regarding "a suggestion about politics and then one about the Navy Department." (Morison, 1323) Roosevelt, after providing some insight into a political matter, came to the business of submarines and more importantly, the men who served on them:

"As to the second matter, I have become greatly interested in submarine boats. They are in no sense substitutes for above-water torpedo boats, not to speak of battleships, cruisers, and the like, but they may on certain occasion supplement other craft, and they should be developed. Now there are excellent old-style naval officers of the kind who drift into positions at Washington who absolutely decline to recognize this fact and who hamper the development of the submarine boat in every way. One of the ways that have done it has been by the absurd and worse than absurd ruling that the officers and men engaged in the very hazardous, delicate, difficult and responsible work of experiment with these submarine boats are not to be considered as on seat duty. I felt positively indignant when I found that the men on the Plunger, who incur a certain risk every time they god down in her and who have to be trained to the highest point as well as to show iron nerve in order to be of any use in their positions, are penalized for being on the Plunger instead of being in some much less responsible and mush less dangerous position on a cruise in a big ship..." (Morison, 1324)

Roosevelt described how the officers had no quarters on board the ship or ashore, or that the men - both enlisted and officers alike - had no messing facilities or other amenities. Roosevelt then outlined certain changes that were to take place. Roosevelt outlined that "enlisted men regularly detailed for instruction in submarine boats but not having qualified shall receive five dollars per month in addition to the pay of their rating...[those who were deemed qualified] shall receive ten dollars per month in addition to the pay of their rating...{and that qualified personnel conducting diving operations] shall receive one dollar in addition to their pay for each day during any part of which they shall have been submerged in a submarine boat while underway." (Morison, 1325) Lastly, Roosevelt explained that adequate repair vessels and materials should be investigated to lessen delays in necessary repairs to the submarines in the fleet. A few weeks later, by an act of executive order, Roosevelt would provide for extra pay to the submariners. It remains in effect to this day.

Chapter 8 - Variations on a Theme

The underwater adventure of President Roosevelt captured the imagination of several writers and the event garnered much media attention. But considering that all were based on different accounts, several variations came to light, even in articles published close to actual event.

A fanciful artistic version of Roosevelt's submarine trip. Author's collection.

In the *Christian Herald* newspaper's September 13, 1905 edition, the front cover illustration, a stereograph by Underwood and Underwood, shows the *U.S.S. Plunger* in the background in what appears to be a photograph. In the foreground there is a line drawing of President Roosevelt, three women, one of which is probably his wife, sitting in front of President Roosevelt and the three women is another male and behind the President are what appear to be two naval officers. The stereograph is interesting though as the background is a photograph of the submarine and some of her crew, with the foreground appearing to be an illustration. The title of the stereograph reads, "President Roosevelt Leaving the *Sylph* to Descend in the *Plunger*."

The article, much like the inaccurate image displayed on the cover, provides an interesting account of the events preceding and the actual dive. The article states that the President "has again shown his fearlessness, as well as his intense interest in everything that pertains to our navy, by going down under the icy waters of Long Island Sound in the new nautical wonder, the submarine torpedo-boat *Plunger*."[39] (*Christian Herald*, 758)

An interesting aspect of this version of events however is provided in the second paragraph where it provides insight into the events leading up to the infamous voyage below the waves. "Several days before actually making the descent, he had been invited to inspect the new craft by her commander, Lieutenant Nelson, who is an expert and enthusiasts on everything that relates to torpedo-boats in general and submarines in particular." (Christian Herald, 758) According to this version, "the President was asked by the lieutenant if he would not like to take a ride with him toward the bottom, and the President stated at once to accept the invitation." But alas, a member of the President's cabinet interjected that "his life was too valuable to his country to be risked that way in a boat that was little better than an experiment." Therefore, the thought of his hands on demonstration was put on hold.

The article then stated that "a few days later Lieutenant Nelson gave a demonstration of the workings of the strange craft near the yacht *Sylph*, and the manoeuvres were eagerly watched by Mrs. Roosevelt and the other members of the President's family. So successful were the evolutions that she was convinced that the President might make the trip in safety." So despite the persistence of members of his Cabinet, ultimately it was report that "Mr. Roosevelt has been held in check by his unwillingness to cause his wife any anxiety."

The middle of the article described the President's trip onboard the *U.S.S. Plunger* with the majority consistent with the *New York Times* article published the day after the event. However, several details are completely

---

[39] I am not sure why the author of the article, which is not listed or known, used the word icy, but the waters of the Long Island Sound are far from icy in August!

different and some could be considered more accurate then originally reported in the *New York Times* article. "Porpoise diving greatly interested the President." In the article published on August 26, 1905, the writer speaks of the President watching porpoise swimming by the conning tower port holes. In the *Christian Herald* article, it explains a different version of what was meant by the concept of "porpoise" diving. "The *Plunger* would dart to the surface, and remain their long enough for the commanding officer to determine the positions of nearby ships, and then plunge instantly below the surface to any desired depth."[40]

Newspaper article showing photographs of the *Plunger* submarine and support vessels during her days in the water's off of Oyster Bay. Author's collection.

---

[40] Hermann Hagedorn would describe both actions – porpoise diving and visits from porpoise – in his version of events.

CHRISTIAN HERALD

SUBSCRIPTION, $1.50 PER ANNUM
PUBLISHED 52 TIMES A YEAR

COPYRIGHT 1905 BY LOUIS KLOPSCH

NEW YORK, SEPTEMBER 13, 1905

28 — NO. 37. PRICE 5 CENTS
ES: BIBLE HOUSE, NEW YORK

Another interesting deviation from the original article was that "President for a while took charge of the button-board, and put the craft through many of her manoeuvres. At one time he pressed the torpedo button, and sent the torpedo, the *Plunger's* only weapon of offense, practically, spinning through space." The *Christian Herald* article also provided post-dive information as the President "discovered that the men of the submarines have been rated as landsmen, and receive twenty percent less pay than regular sailors. He has given orders to have this inequality rectified, for he believes that there is no branch of our military service that is as dangerous as that of the crews of the submarines, either in peace or in war."

The *Daily Northwestern*, Saturday Evening edition, published an abbreviated Associated Press article on August 26, 1905, under the title, "Tests of the Plunger." The article was quick to point out that Roosevelt's under sea jaunt had thus "endeared himself to the naval offices and men the world over and made Lieut. Charles Nelson, commander of the *Plunger*, the proudest and happiest man in the United States navy." The *Arizona Republican* and *Fort Wayne Journal-Gazette* of the same date also explained that "rain descended in torrents and a northeaster whipped the surface of the waters with big rollers," but that below the surface the little craft was "quiet and peaceful where the President sat as any easy parlor chair would be." The *Fort Wayne Journal-Gazette* further explained that the "secrecy maintained by the president" was able to be maintained thanks to the inclement weather that had provide the *U.S.S. Plunger* with "practically the entire Long Island Sound to herself." Various newspapers covered the historic event and their titles for the much used Associated Press article varied:

Roosevelt Dives Beneath Billows – *The Constitution*, Atlanta, GA.

The President Takes Plunge in Submarine – *Gazette and Bulletin*, Williamsport, PA

Roosevelt Under Sea – *Marion Daily Star*, Marion, Ohio

Chief Takes a Dive – *The Daily Courier*, Connellsville, PA

President Goes to Bottom of Ocean – *The Fort Wayne Sentinel*, FT. Wayne, IN.

Roosevelt Is Under Waves of Ocean For Fifty Minutes – *Post-Standard*, Syracuse, NY

At Bottom of Sound – *The Washington Post*, Washington, DC

Some of the newspapers even included illustrations of the event and of the submarine. The *Massillon Independent – Semi Weekly*, included an illustration of a "Submarine Attacking a Battleship," which of course was not part of the President's review, but certainly interesting none the less. The *Fort Wayne Sentinel* included two photographs showing the "submarine boat in which President Roosevelt went to the Bottom of the Sea," with a photograph of the *U.S.S. Plunger* being towed by the Navy Tug *Apache* and also a photograph of the *U.S.S. Plunger*'s stern while performing on a "trail trip at the Brooklyn Navy Yard." The *Post-Standard* of Syracuse, New York, also ran the same photograph but did not indicate that it was at Brooklyn, but rather that it was a view of the submarine that Roosevelt had "explored at length the bottom of Oyster Bay."

Chapter 9 - Shots across the Bow

Though the majority of the media coverage was positive and exciting, there of course were those who decided to weigh in on the event and take a shot at the commander in Chief and his actions below the surface onboard the *U.S.S. Plunger*. On August 27, 1905, just two days after the President's historic underwater adventure, *The Constitution*, published in Atlanta, Georgia provided an editorial to its readers titled, "The Submarine's Greatest Triumph." The editorial pointed out that the trip may "well be regarded a great triumph for this novel type of fighting machine," but that "curiosity got the better of discretion," and President Roosevelt should not have taken such a great risk. It continued that when the idea of Roosevelt going onboard and more dangerously below the surface, on the torpedo boat, a "chorus of friendly protest" had been raised. In accordance with those who opposed the dangerous feat, on many occasions, Roosevelt had stated that he had "no intention to accept the hospitality of the *Plunger* and its commander," by taking the plunge himself.

Though the review and hand's on experience had been successful, the editorial concluded that the writer and therefore the reader should not "being ourselves to entirely forgive President Roosevelt for taking such great chances. Think what it would have meant for the country if things had gone wrong and we had been inflicted with a Fairbanks as president." As the last comment was read, I wondered if more resentment existed due to Roosevelt's gamble or the gamble of the man who would have succeeded him if something had gone wrong.

Interestingly enough, a small tidbit of information on the same page from *The Constitution*'s same issue also addressed the President's trip. "The superstitious sailors felt no fear when they knew President Roosevelt was going down in the submarine boat with them. That man will always come to the surface again." In other words, the United States Navy was behind the President and they would be damned to think a lowly submarine could keep Roosevelt quiet or complacent in his affairs.

The *New York Times* on August 27, 1905 also offered an editorial titled "Our Submerged President," in which, once again, a similar argument was offered. The article pointed out that "there is an appreciable element of peril in the submarine at the present stage of its evolution," but even though the technology was not perfected as of yet, and it was this "element of irresistible attractiveness," that drove Roosevelt's actions. It continued to provide a thought that Roosevelt was welcomed to do whatever he wished to do as a private citizen, but at the time, he was not a private citizen, but rather the leader of "eighty million people." The thought that he would continue to entrust his life to some "new-fangled, submersible, collapsible, or otherwise dangers device," was the major concern posed.

To further exemplify the point of fearlessness, the editorial continued that "we have no doubt that the President is secretly aching to soar in that yellow sausage which has been floating over Manhattan in these later days," referring to some sort of balloon or aircraft over the New York skyline. It continued that "it is most fortunate that the aerial machine in question will hold but one, because if it held two the President would insist upon being the other." At the conclusion of the article, the writer stated that Roosevelt should "restrain himself from doing those stunts of adventure," and remember his solemn duty as president.

On August 29, in the editorial section of the *Colorado Springs Gazette*, under the title, "The President and the Plunger," it stated that "we are all glad that our President is a strenuous individual who is afraid of nothing under the sun," but that it might be better for him to restrain his "dare-devil exploits to hunting mountain lions and violators of the law and the submarine boats to the men for whom they are built." Even though a published denial of such a plan had been published by a multitude of papers, Roosevelt insisted on taking the dip beneath the water.

Though the article conceded that a submerged trip onboard a submarine did not exactly mean certain death, it was certainly not an activity free of peril or death. It reminded readers that the British had lost a submarine with the loss of several men a year previously and that "only a few weeks" previously, the French submarine boat *Farfadet* had become "disabled in the Mediterranean waters and her entire crew of some thirty men perished." The editorial concluded by stating that Roosevelt was welcomed to do what he needed to do to satisfy his "dare-devil instincts" but that as president he should not be indulging in "such foolhardy pastimes as going to the bottom of the sea in a submarine boat."

The *Agitator* newspaper of Wellsboro, Pennsylvania published a similar editorial on Wednesday, August 30, 1905. After a thorough review of previously made arguments, the editorial quickly pointed out that there were "so many problems above the water level for our Chief Magistrate to grapple with that it does seem foolhardy for him to be exploring the bottom of Oyster Bay." But interestingly it concluded by stating that "nobody knows what President Roosevelt is going to do next." Articles published the same day in other papers would dare to ask that very question.

As if going under the waves in an "untested" craft wasn't bad enough and as editorial writers expressed their dissatisfaction with President Roosevelt's undersea adventure aboard the *U.S.S. Plunger*, they must have gasped when they heard that aeronaut A. Roy Knabenshue was contemplating the idea to extend an invitation to the President to go aloft in an airship. According to the article published in the *Fort Wayne Weekly Sentinel* on Wednesday, August 30, 1905, he was quoted stating that he was only hesitating "because I don't want the president to think I am too forward. If nothing happens I shall extend this invitation with a few weeks." But the invitation would not be for both to pilot the airship but rather the Toledo native aeronaut explained that "it would not be safe for two to try the trip, but I have the greatest confidence in Mr. Roosevelt being able to sail it alone."

Knabenshue was heading for Manhattan to test his skills as an actor and explained that though he had excited and thrilled audiences with his airship activities in both New York and in the Mid-west, he was cautious as to the future of the airship business. The business, he explained, "costs a lot of money," and that he wanted to warn people "inclined to invest money in airship companies that there is absolutely no chance of the airship being of any value in a commercial way for years." Ultimately, the thought of the invitation would remain just an invitation.[41] The President's descent in the *U.S.S. Plunger* however, had precipitated the aeronaut's idea.

---

[41] Roosevelt would ascend in an aircraft piloted by Arch Hoxsey on October 10, 1910. Roosevelt was airborne for approximately four minutes. Hoxsey died in a plane crash two and a half months later. (Theodore Roosevelt Association) A photograph showing Roosevelt and Hoxsey in the aircraft is on view at the Cradle of Aviation Museum, Long Island, New York.

Chapter 10 - Advocate for a Naval Hero

During Roosevelt's first term as president, Secretary of the Navy, John Moody was reminded that no marker or grave for one of the United States' greatest naval heroes, John Paul Jones, stood in Paris. Certainly monuments existed in the nation for which he had fought so heroically, but his final resting place – in an unknown location – in France remained unmarked. Moody, realizing the importance and significance of this shortcoming responded in a New York Times article on September 17, 1903 that if "the bones of the distinguished naval hero can be found... [he would] order a warship to France to bring them home." Moody circumvented the lack of a grave marker in France by the statement, but first Commodore Jones' remains would first have to be found.

Returning Jones to America became a priority for both the United States Navy and the United States Government. On November 19th, 1903, Representative Rainey of Illinois "introduced a resolution...instructing the Secretary of State to locate, disinter, and bring to the United States for burial at Arlington National Cemetery" the remains which then allegedly rested "in the old Protestant Cemetery" in Paris, France. (*NYT*, 20NOV1903) The appropriation of ten thousand dollars was authorized for the resolution however a major stumbling block remained in the path of Jones' return. The old Protestant Cemetery was occupied by physical structures. The resolution, cognizant of this fact included provisions that the Secretary of State "to secure options on all the property and submit the same to Congress, that it may be purchased, the buildings removed, and the place suitably improved and marked." (*NYT*, 20NOV1903) Nothing was to stand in the way of Commodore Jones' last voyage across the Atlantic Ocean.

The following April, the Daughters of the American Revolution voiced their support of the plan at their national convention in Washington, DC. The leadership and members of the organization agreed to the formation of a committee to press upon members of Congress to fund the finding and return of

Commodore Jones. In addition to forming the committee, the organization also raised an additional twenty-five thousand dollars to assist in the process.

By the following year President Roosevelt voiced his opinion of the search and process and echoed the previous sentiment regarding the importance of returning Jones to the country that he had so bravely fought. During a session of Congress on February 13, 1905, Roosevelt explained updates that he had received from the U.S. Ambassador to France, Porter, regarding his efforts in locating the commodore's remains. In addition to the report of Porter's progress, Roosevelt also urged Congress to appropriate funds for monuments for "both Paul Jones and John Barry to emphasize the value set by our people upon the naval commanders in our War for Independence." (*NYT*, 14FEB1905) Roosevelt also reminded Congress that not only did he support Ambassador Porter's efforts, but that he too wanted to see the money set aside for the project. Roosevelt continued stating that "the great interest which our people feel in the story of Paul Jones' life, the National sense of gratitude for the great service done by him toward the achievement of independence and the sentiment....regret felt because the body of one of our greatest heroes lies forgotten and unmarked in foreign soil, lead me to approve the Ambassador's suggestion that Congress should take advantage of this unexpected opportunity to do the proper honor to the memory of Paul Jones and appropriate the sum of $35,000, or so much thereof as may be necessary for the purposes above described to be extended under direction of the Secretary of State." (*NYT*, 14FEB1905) Roosevelt had not mixed words. It was clearly evident that he, like many others, wanted Jones returned to American soil.

Approximately ten days after Roosevelt's impassioned plea to Congress, a metal casket which was "believed to contain the bones of John Paul Jones" had been recovered "16 feet below a grain shed at 14 Rue Grange aux Belies." (*NYT*, 25FEB1905) A copper name plate was affixed to the coffin, however upon initial closer inspection, the plate was "so time worn as to be undecipherable." (*NYT*, 25FEB1905) On the same day as the coffin's discovery was made public, in a special to the *New York Times*, it was reported that the President's February 13th call to action by the Congress for the project was likely to be in the form of "an item…inserted in one of the appropriation bills to meet the necessary expenditure." (*NYT*, 25FEB1905) The contents of the retrieved coffin would remain a mystery for only a short time.

John Paul Jones. Courtesy U.S. Navy.

The initially undecipherable name plate on the coffin was identified by the 26th of the same month. Upon closer inspection it was determined that the coffin contained an Englishman who had been buried on May 5, 1790, "two years before the death of Jones." (*NYT*, 27FEB1905) Though Jones' coffin had not yet been found, the discovery was integral to the search because it "established the fact that those buried in the Protestant cemetery about the time of Jones' death lie in the vicinity of where the search was commencing." (*NYT*, 27FEB1905) The search continued.

76

On April 14th, 1905, after an additional month of digging and searching, Ambassador Porter informed the State Department that he felt confident that he had been successful in the location of Jones' remains. Congress was once again asked to support the project which in its absence of financial support, had been funded by Ambassador Porter. (*NYT*, 15APR1905) The final resting place however, remained in doubt. After a conference between Secretary Morton and Acting Secretary Loomis it was determined that Jones would be returned to the United States by a "naval vessel with a proper convoy." (*NYT*, 18APR1905) Where the body would be interred however, remained in doubt. Initial thoughts felt that Arlington National Cemetery would be his final resting place; however, a decision had not yet been determined. It would be up to President Roosevelt to intervene a few days later as the State and Navy Departments volleyed their reasoning behind their intentions for his final interment. The State Department believed that he should be placed at Arlington, whereas the Navy stated that they desired that he be "entombed in the National Sailors' Cemetery, at Annapolis." (*NYT*, 23APR1905) In addition to a place at Arlington and Annapolis, there were other locations that also were "claiming the right to Jones' burial place" including "New York, Philadelphia, and Fredericksburg, Va." (*NYT*, 23APR1905) As the country waited for news on where the famed hero of the revolution would be final entombed, "Admiral Dewey, in a letter addressed to Mrs. Elizabeth C. Williams, a member of the Daughters of the American Revolution....expressed himself as being in favor of depositing the remains at Arlington." (*NYT*, 23APR1905) The admiral's opinion aside, it would be up to Roosevelt to administer the final call in the much debated outcome. Roosevelt, "followed these proceedings with keen interest, recognizing the propaganda value for the United States Navy, which he was trying to make the strongest in the world as Paul Jones had predicted it would become." (Morison, 410)

While the matter continued to be contested in the various halls of government, John Paul Jones underwent a series of preservation treatments while he lay in the Ecole de Medecin, in Paris, France. Porter, who was near the end of his appointment as Ambassador to France, remarked in a dispatch to the State Department that:

> *"Finding that the body showed some signs of changing in appearance from exposure to the air, as soon as the examinations were completed at the Ecole de Medecin with a preparation which I am assured will prevent any deterioration. The body was then redressed in the shirt and sheet in so as not to be injured by shocks in transportation, and replaced in its original coffin...This was inclosed [sp] in a leaden casket with a plate glass showing the head and chest, and hermitically closed. Seals were then affixed in such manner that it could not be opened without breaking them. This was placed in an outer coffin of oak, and on the twentieth (April) the remains were transferred from the School of Medicine to the American Church of the Holy Trinity and placed in the receiving vault, where the body lies covered with the American flag." (NYT, 2MAY1905)*

Porter was also questioned by several of the cities vying for the honor to bury Jones to which he deferred the final judgment of Jones' final port to the "National Government for decision." (*NYT*, 2MAY1905) Regarding the body of Jones, a clerk at the American Embassy, A. Beisel who viewed the body at the Ecole de Medecin remarked that Jones' features were "wonderfully well preserved, the features bearing an expression of sleeping and that he considered it "a great honor that that the task of sealing the remains" fell upon him. (*NYT*, 2MAY1905)

Two months later, Admiral John Paul Jones finally returned to the country to which he had so valiantly fought for during the Revolutionary War. Roosevelt ordered four cruisers including the "U.S.S. *Brooklyn* (flying the flag of Rear Admiral Charles D. Sigsbee), *Tacoma*, *Chattanooga*, and *Galveston*…to bring his body home." (Morison, 411) After a full military honor was bestowed upon the coffin by French and United States Naval personnel, the casket of Jones was laid to rest temporarily, in an "unpretentious vault in the centre of the

78

grounds of the Naval Academy."[42] An armed guard was placed outside the vault where the casket was placed while the unfinished chapel of the service academy continued to be built.[43] Though Roosevelt was not present during the transfer from ship to shore, he would be on hand less than a year later when the remains were transferred to a crypt "beneath the grand marble stairway of Bancroft Hall" at Annapolis on August 24, 1906. (*NYT*, 25APR1906) With vessels of the United States Naval fleet in the background, Roosevelt spoke to a crowd of over ten thousand who had gathered for the event. His speech echoed his longstanding commitment to the United States Navy and to the importance of leadership in the naval ranks. After thanking the French government and navy for their assistance, Roosevelt acknowledged the distinguished guests in attendance at the event. Roosevelt stated:

> *"The future naval officers who live within these walls will find in the career of the man whose life we this day celebrate not merely a subject for admiration and respect, but an object lesson to be taken into their innermost hearts. Every officer in our navy should know by heart the deeds of John Paul Jones. Every officer in our navy should feel in each fibre[sp] of his being the eager desire to emulate the energy, the professional capacity, the indomitable determination, and the dauntless scorn of death with marked John Paul Jones above all his fellows. The history of our navy like the history of our nation, only extends over a period of a century and a quarter yet we already have many memories of pride to thrill us as we read and hear of what had been done by our fighting men of the sea, from*

---

[42] Two days prior to John Paul Jones' return to American soil, on July 21, 1905, the United States Navy gunboat *Bennington* suffered a terrible boiler explosion in San Diego, California, which killed sixty men. (Sweetman, 120)

[43] During this time frame, Roosevelt received a petition including the signatures of 30,000 citizens urging that the *U.S.S. Constitution*, better known as *Old Ironsides*, be saved. Roosevelt "suggested that the old frigate be rigged and equipped as she appeared in her fighting days and sent to Annapolis." Though no determination was made at the delivery of the 170 foot long petition, Roosevelt suggested that the petition be "placed on exhibition in the Navy Department in connection with a model of the *Constitution*." The *U.S.S. Constitution* remains a part of the United States Naval Fleet to this day. (*NYT*, 21JAN1906)

Perry and MacDonough to Farragut and Dewey. Thee
memories include brilliant victories, and also, now and
then, defeats only less honorable than the victories
themselves, but the only defeats in which we can praise
can be given are those where, against heavy odds, men
have stood to the death in hopeless battle."

Roosevelt then proceeded to remind the audience of John Paul Jones'
spirited remarks "I have not yet begun to fight" speech from the deck of the
Bonhomme Richard to the *Serepis*. He also recounted the daring yet unfortunate
loss of Captain Morris and his vessel *Cumberland*, "when summoned to
surrender, Morris replied, 'Never, I'll sink alongside' and made his words good."
Roosevelt then shifted from historical to the importance of the United States
Naval Academy and future officers:

"Let every midshipman who passes through this
institution remember, as he looks upon the tomb of John
Paul Jones, that while no courage can atone for the lack
of that efficiency which comes only through careful
preparation in advance through careful training of the
men and careful fitting out of the engines of war yet that
none of these things can avail unless in the moment of
crisis the heart rises level with the crisis."

To the American people, Roosevelt explained that:

"I wish that our people as a whole, and especially those
among us who occupy high legislative or administrative
positions, would study the history of our nation, not
merely for the purpose of National self-gratification, but
with the desire to learn the lessons that history teaches.
Let the men who talk lightly about its being unnecessary
for us now to have an army and navy adequate for the
work of this Nation in the World remember that such
utterances are not merely foolish, for in their effects they
may at any time be fraught with disaster and disgrace to
the Nation's honor as well as disadvantages to its
interests."

Roosevelt then focused in on the historical teachings of the War of 1812. Having written and study the naval engagements of the second war with the British, Roosevelt was able to draw some distinct parallels between those in government positions in the post-Revolutionary War years to the years following the Spanish-American War – especially those who scoffed at the building up and strengthening of the United States Naval fleet.

> *"Let them take to hear some of the lessons which should be learned by the study of the war of 1812. As a people we are too apt to remember that some of our ships did well in that war. We had a few ships – a very few ships- and they did so well as to show the utter folly of not having enough of them. Thanks to our folly as a Nation, thanks to the folly that found expression in the views of those at the seat of Government, not a ship of any importance had been built with a dozen years before the war began, and the navy was so small that when once the war was on, our opponents were able to establish a close blockade throughout the length of our coast, so that not a ship could go from one port to another, and all traffic had to go on land. Our parsimony in not preparing an adequate navy (which would have prevented the war) coast in the end literally thousands of dollars for every one dollar thus foolishly saved. After two years of that war an utterly inconsiderable British force of about 4,000 men were landed here in the bay, defeated with ease a larger body of raw troops put against it, and took Washington. I am sorry to say that those of our countrymen who now speak of these deeds usually confine themselves to denouncing the British for having burned certain buildings in Washington. They had better spare their breaths."*

It was apparent to all in attendance that Roosevelt was not mixing any words regarding the necessity for both a strong navy and army to protect the United States. He continued:

> *"The sin of the invaders in burning the buildings is trivial compared with the sin of our own people in failing to make ready an adequate force to defeat the attempt. This Nation was guilty of such short-*

81

sightedness, of such folly, of such lack of preparation that it was forced supinely to submit to the insult and was impotent to avenge it...Let us remember our own shortcomings, and see to it that the men in public life to-day are not permitted to bring about a state of things by which we should in effect invite a repetition of such a humiliation."

Roosevelt then charged the cadre of the Navy in accordance with his charge to the audience, especially those in public office who, in their charge of responsibility, determined the fate of the defensive and offensive effectiveness of the armed forces.[44]

"Let you in the navy remember that you must do your part. You will be worthless in war if you have not prepared yourselves for it in peace. You will be utterly unable to rise in the needs of the crisis if you have not by long years of steady and patient work fitted yourselves to get the last ounce of work out of every man, every gun, and every ship in the fleet; if you have not practiced on the high seas until each ship can do its best, can show at its best alone, or in conjunction with others in fleet formation. Remember that no courage can atone for lack of that preparedness..."

Roosevelt relinquished the stage to a host of other speakers. Upon their completed remarks, the casket containing John Paul Jones was marched to the Bancroft Hall, followed by Roosevelt and other dignitaries. After the coffin was placed below the stairs, a brief prayer was provide by a military chaplain. Roosevelt returned to his automobile and with an escort of cavalry and

---

[44] Roosevelt had addressed the cadets at Annapolis in 1902. "It cannot be too often repeated that in modern war, and especially modern naval war, the chief factor in achieving triumph is what has been done in the way of thorough preparation and training before the beginning of war...Officers and men alike must have the sea habit; officers and men alike must realize that in battle the only shots that count are the shots that hit and that normally the victory will lie with the side whose shots hit oftenest. Seamanship and marksmanship – these must be the two prime objects of your training, both for yourselves and for the men under you." (*Book of the Navy*, 298) *The Book of the Navy*, published during the Second World War included the following – Dedicated to the Memory of THEODORE ROOSEVELT who loved fighting ships, knew well how to write about them, and was the great protagonist of the modern United States Navy.

"battalions of midshipmen," he went to Admiral Sims' residence and then returned shortly thereafter to the train station where he boarded a train for Washington. One of the heroes of the Revolution had finally been returned to the land that he had so valiantly fought for over a hundred and twenty years earlier.[45] Roosevelt, his message sent clear and concisely, returned to his helm to continue to steer a course for a stronger, more efficient, and powerful United States Navy.[46]

---

[45] John Paul Jones was moved into the crypt of the United States Naval Academy Chapel on January 26, 1913. See *Appendix D* for additional information.

[46] According to Morison in *John Paul Jones: A Sailor's Biography* - though various places had requested to be honored by having Jones interred in their town, "Congress, guided emphatically by President Roosevelt, decided that the most appropriate spot would be the crypt of the chapel of the Naval Academy, whose establishment Jones had urged and predicted." (Morison, 412)

Chapter 11 - Foundations of a Naval Legacy

Roosevelt supported multiple aspects of the United States Navy including the importance of the naval militias during his first presidential term. He would not waver from that course for the duration of this second term and in the post-White House years. Roosevelt reiterated his position on the need for strong and effective militias on January 14, 1904 when he spoke to the National Association of Naval Militia which was holding their meeting in Washington, D.C.

> *"It is not necessary for me to say to a body like this that the position of the United States as a great world power, and her ability to maintain with dignity and self-respect her position in the world at large, depend primarily upon the efficiency of her navy, and that you, by the work you do in the naval militia, can contribute as no other body of civilians on land can possibly contribute to make that efficiency reach a high standard." (NYT, 15JAN1904)*

In October of that same year, as Roosevelt prepared for the coming elections, he "forgot the campaign for an hour...and had a long talk on battleships, cruisers, navies and war...with Sir William White, R.N., a world famous naval architect." (*NYT*, 13OCT1904) White, who was visiting Washington, had stopped by to "pay his respects to Secretary of the Navy Morton," when Morton suggested visiting the White House. (*NYT*, 13OCT1904)

Though initially busy with other commitments, Roosevelt cleared his afternoon schedule to talk ships and navies. In the room for the discussion were Admirals Dewey, Converse, Capps, Evans, and Rodgers. Though the top of the United States Navy pyramid was present, the "President took a leading part in the discussion. In fact Sir White was surprised by the technical knowledge displayed by Mr. Roosevelt in his searching inquiries about naval architecture." (*NYT*, 13OCT1904) White at the conclusion of the meeting provided his view of the current status of the United States Navy stating "comparing its new ships with

84

those of France, Germany, and Great Britain….[he was of the opinion] that the battleships now building in this country stood at the front of the best types of the modern battleship." (*NYT*, 13OCT1904)

President Roosevelt after his inaugural address in 1905. Author's collection.

After his election to his second term Roosevelt was quick to again reiterate his position on the importance of the U.S. Navy. In an address at the commemoration of George Washington's birthday at the University of Pennsylvania on February 23, 1905, Roosevelt stated:

> *"Never since the beginning of our country's history has the navy been used in an unjust war. Never has it failed to render great and sometimes vital service to the Republic. It has not been too strong for our good, though often not strong enough to do all the good it should have done. Our possession of the Philippines, our interest in the trade of the Orient, our building the Isthmian Canal, our insistence upon the Monroe Doctrine, all demand that our navy shall be of adequate size and for its size o unsurpassed efficiency. If it is strong enough I believe it will minimize the chance of our being drawn into foreign war. If we let it run down it is as certain as the day that sooner or later we shall have to choose between a probably disastrous foreign war or a peace kept on the terms that imply National humiliation." (NYT, 23FEB1905)*

Roosevelt continued explaining his concept of peace through a show of force:

> *"Our navy is the surest guaranty of peace and the cheapest insurance against war, and those who in whatever capacity have helped to build it up during the past twenty years have been in good faith observing and living up to one of the most important principles which Washington laid down for the guidance of his countrymen. Nor was Washington the only one of our great Presidents who showed farsighted patriotism by support of the navy."[47] (NYT, 23FEB1905)*

---

[47] Roosevelt also took the opportunity to show the "farsighted patriotism" of other including Andrew Jackson. While in Congress, "Andrew Jackson voted for the first warships we ever built as part of our regular navy; and he voted against the grant of money to pay our humiliating tribute to the pirates of the Barbary States. Old Hickory was a patriot through and through, and there was not an ounce of timidity in his nature, and of course he felt only indignant contempt for a policy which purchased an ignoble peace by cowardice instead of a expecting a just peace by showing we were as little willing to submit to as to inflict aggression. Had a majority of Jackson's colleagues and

A few months later, after his submarine adventure, Roosevelt continued his vocal and active support of the U.S. Navy. After the plunge beneath the murky waters of the Long Island Sound in late August 1905, Theodore Roosevelt acted quickly to address a major concern regarding the submariner's world which was chronicled in a special report to the *New York Times* on August 27, 1905. Roosevelt expressed that he was "thoroughly delighted with his submarine exhibition," and that the review had provided a "fulfillment of wishes entertained by him ever since the submarine boat became a part of the American Navy." The articled explained that Roosevelt had previously been "dissuaded from going down in a Holland boat at Annapolis by members of the Cabinet." Ultimately, the commander in chief did not allow any dissuasion from the unique opportunity of going on board the *U.S.S. Plunger* in the home waters of the summer White House.

"I never spent a more enjoyable and interesting afternoon in all my life," President Roosevelt explained, "the working of every one of the intricate appliances on board the *Plunger* and the assurance with which the crew performed their difficult duties even when the interior of the boat was plunged in perfect darkness was a revelation to me." But the afternoon under the waves was more than just an escape to the undersea realm in an effort to fulfill Roosevelt's curiosity in submarine boats, but rather there was an impression by those close to the President that the event would "usher in a new era of this important branch of the navy," which had previously received little better than "stepmotherly treatment at the hands of the naval authorities."

Roosevelt wasted no time and facilitated change almost immediately. He learned that submarine crews were considered as land based sailors which meant that they received "25 per cent less then the men regularly assigned duty on naval

---

successors felt as he did about the navy, had it been built up instead of being brought to a standstill, it would probably never have been necessary to fight the war of 1812." (*NYT*, 23FEB1905)

87

ships." In addition to the lower wages, despite the added risks of submarine duty, the submariners were less regarded for promotion. As of the following morning, the United States Navy was ordered to initiate change by "placing the men employed on the submarines on the regular roll with the men doing duty on shipboard." This monumental change exists to this day.

Another facet not be overlooked was the admiration of the President gained by the crew of the *U.S.S. Plunger* as a result of his "in the trenches visit," and presidential review. The article expressed that the "men on board the *Plunger* spoke in terms of admiration of the President and his behavior during the hour spent with them far beneath the surface of the Sound." Nelson added that "the President stood it as well as any of us and that means a good deal for conditions in a submerged submarine boat involve inconvenience and distress to the man accustomed to it, and much more to a landsman." Roosevelt showed that he was willing to do what he had asked his men to do and they would never forget it.

Roosevelt would continue his support of the United States Navy throughout his presidency. There are several examples of Roosevelt's willingness to roll up his sleeves with enlisted sailors while either visiting or reviewing the Navy and its vessel. In an article titled, "Roosevelt Shoveled Coal on Big Cruiser," published in the *New York Times* on November 1st, 1905, he had been on board the cruiser *West Virginia* and during his inspection of the vessel, he toured the engine room. "He showed great interest in the stokers who were working under pressure to keep the cruiser up to the fast gait," and the men presented the President with a ceremonial shovel. When they asked him to use the shovel to "throw a few heaps of coal on the fire," he smiled, took the shovel, "dug deep into the pile of coal and then swung and thrust for another round and then passed the shovel to each of the remaining stokers who then added a shovelful to the blaze." Once all in the compartment has used the special shovel, "it was smashed into a thousand pieces, which were distributed for souvenirs." In addition the boiler where all of this activity had transpired was named "Roosevelt."

But Roosevelt did more than just roll up his sleeves with the men; he also gave them a rousing speech. Throughout his address, Roosevelt explained that 'it was a privilege for any President to come aboard a squadron of American warships such as these, not alone to see the ships, but to see the men who handle them." He expressed how every "American should be proud," of what he had witnessed while on board, shoulder to shoulder with both the officers and enlisted men alike." Roosevelt praised the seriousness and determination that each man on board had exemplified. He explained the obligation of the Navy to train in peace to be ready for war and that each man must continue to adhere to his duties to prepare for the worst. In closing, Roosevelt remarked that "no other nation can boast a better squadron, a squadron composed of more formidable vessels," and that though only the *U.S.S. Colorado* had completed a review of gunnery practice, he reminded the men that "battles are decided by gunfire and that the only shots that count are the shots that hit."

On September 3, 1906, Roosevelt and many dignitaries viewed the awesome might of the United States Navy during a presidential review in the waters of the Long Island Sound. "Twelve great battleships, eight powerful cruisers, four monitors, twelve destroyers and torpedo boats, five auxiliary cruisers, three submarines, and a troopship – forty-five craft in all, a ship of war for every State in the Union – lay in three long columns within sight of the Sound's green shore, while the President's yacht *Mayflower*, with Mr. Roosevelt" steamed between the fleet. (*NYT*, 4SEP1906)[48] Thousands of others lined the shores of Long Island and puttered about in dinghies or lazed about in their yachts, gawking at the awesome display of the Atlantic fleet. Roosevelt commented in regards to the show of force that "any man who fails to be

---

[48] One of the submarines was the *U.S.S. Porpoise*, one of the *U.S.S. Plunger*'s sister submarines. According to the *New York Times* article, Lieutenant C.P. Nelson was in command. (*NYT*, 4SEP1906)

patriotically inspired by such a sight as this is a mighty poor American, and every American who has seen it ought to be a better American for it." (*NYT*, 4SEP1906) As the *Mayflower* transited between the ships, Roosevelt declared to the dignitaries, which included members of the Committee on Naval Affairs that they were "responsible for it. It is your handiwork, and it has all been done within the past ten years. Every one of these ships is a fighter and ready to go into action at a moment's notice. Again, you have shown your wisdom in the appropriations for target practice, for there is where the American Navy excels. Our men can shoot, and shoot straight, and therein lies our naval strength and our superiority." (*NYT*, 4SEP1906)

The day long event was hugely popular, but its location – in the waters of the Long Island Sound – had raised some concern. On August 25, 1906, a year after his plunge in the submarine in the same body of water, an editorial was published in the *New York Times* titled The Naval Review. The editorial questioned the location of the review and called upon the President to change the venue so tat more of the public could view the review. "To the south shore [of Long Island], off Coney Island, or off the Rockaway Beaches there are miles of standing room, miles of even 'board walk,' which would afford hundreds of thousands, one may safely say millions of spectators the opportunity of seeing what the President eagerly desires as many as possible of his countrymen to see." (*NYT*, 25AUG1906)

The editorial, though partly back-handed in his obvious lack of agreement in the location for the review, was complimentary regarding Roosevelt's efforts in supporting and building the United States Navy. "Should the President be convinced that it is not good for him or for us that the American Navy should be treated or regarded as his personal plaything, but rather as a National possession and a source of national pride?" (*NYT*, 25AUG1906) Soon after this comment however a true compliment and observation surfaced amidst the black and white written scolding. "The navy which, within a short human

90

memory, has grown to its material from a collection of antiquated hulks to a modern fleet, the second, third, or fourth as it may be, among the navies of the World." To Roosevelt specifically the editorial explained that "the President has himself, by speech and pen… [has identified] the importance of the navy, and striven, greatly to his credit, to bring the people of the United States to an appreciation of its actual formidableness and its value. We can recall no other American who either as a private author or as a public official has done so much in that direction." The call to change the location of the review remained. The article and its vocal call for change fell on deaf ears. For the second time in three years, Roosevelt would welcome a naval review, in the waters near his home, Sagamore Hill.[49]

Another example of Roosevelt's heartfelt admiration and respect for the United States Navy occurred while he was on board the *U.S.S. Missouri* after a review of gunnery exercises from the battleships *Maine*, *Missouri*, *Illinois*, *Alabama*, *Kearsarge*, and *Iowa*.[50] The demonstration, profiled in an article published on September 30, 1906, was to show the President, "as fully as possible the workings of modern ships of war under fighting conditions." After the spectacular program was completed, Roosevelt, who had traveled 250 miles by sea to witness the exercise, decided to sit down with the crew of the *Missouri* for dinner. A surprise to both the officers and enlisted men of the ship, Roosevelt and his guests sat down at a table amongst the crew. One sailor quickly realized

---

[49] On August 17, 1903, Roosevelt held a presidential review of the fleet. Roosevelt and "half a hundred guests, including leading military and naval commanders of the United States; a company of Naval Attaches of foreign nations, watched the North Atlantic Fleet consisting of four battleships, eight cruisers and ten torpedo boats destroyers." Toward the end of the review, two torpedo boats, the *Decatur* and *Barry* rammed one another at approximately twenty-two knots. The celebration of September 3, 1906 was less eventful.
[50] Not every U.S. Navy "Jack" was endeared to Roosevelt. One such sailor, Arthur Jenkins, was "arrested by order of the Secretary of the Navy and placed in the brig of the receiving ship *Franklin*…[on] the charge of having sent an offensive card to President Roosevelt in Washington." (*NYT*, 16AUG1908) The card which was described as "saucy' was finally made public in late September 1908, though attempts to find out what was inscribed on the card have met with negative results. (*NYT*, 23SEP1908)

that the President and his guests did not have napkins at their table and "rushed to the wardroom to procure the necessary table linen." Upon the sailors return to the table, President Roosevelt thanked him but explained that he was "dining with the boys to-day." He continued that he would not have any "privileges which they did not enjoy." As the sailors, President, and his guests dined, no further action, besides eating was taken. At the conclusion of dinner a group of sailors presented the "President's table with a box of cigars." Needless to say, the moment of dining with the crew of the ship had a lasting impression for both officers and enlisted men alike. It was this willingness to be amongst his men that must have endeared the men of the United States Navy to their commander-in-chief.

But Roosevelt's long standing legacy in regards to the United States Navy was not relegated to Presidential reviews and mid-day meals amongst the enlisted crews. Roosevelt, during his two administrations provided an open sea of possibilities to the maritime branch of the armed services. During a speech at the Merchant's Club in Chicago on May 10th, 1905, after addressing the group regarding the importance of business leaders knowing how to be trustworthy, Roosevelt reflected upon the importance of presidential views. "I need not say to those of you who know anything of me at all that I believe in a big navy, and I hope I need not say that I believe it is as a provocative to war, but as a guarantee of peace." (*NYT*, 11MAY1905) He continued to explain that "we cannot abandon our position on the Monroe Doctrine; we cannot abandon the Panama Canal; we cannot abandon the duties that have come to us from the mere fact of our growth as a nation, from the growth of our commercial interests in the East and in the West, on the Atlantic and on the Pacific." (*NYT*, 11MAY1905)[51]

---

[51] Roosevelt also made an address to the members of the Hamilton Club in Chicago on the same day. Regarding the importance of their namesake: "You, by your name, commemorate a great statesman – Hamilton – one of the most brilliant and one of the greatest constructive statesmen of the era of constructive statesmanship: a man to whom this republic owes a well-nigh incalculable debt." (*NYT*, 11MAY1905) Alexander

Though some historians would argue the long term planning aspect of President Roosevelt's naval strategy, it is hard to argue the impact of the Atlantic Fleet during its historic circumnavigation of the Globe.

Hamilton's vision established the Revenue Cutter Service, one of the agencies that provided the foundation for the United States Coast Guard, in 1790.

Chapter 12 - The Atlantic Fleet

Roosevelt boarded the *Mayflower* and headed down the Potomac to be a part of the 300th anniversary celebration of the founding of Jamestown in the early morning hours of April 26, 1907. Along with his guests, Roosevelt took part in the exposition that featured, among other spectacles, a naval fleet including thirty-eight United States naval vessels and twelve foreign flagged naval vessels, all "dressed in the best of their festival bunting." (NYT, 27APR1907) After the naval review was completed by Roosevelt and his distinguished guests, he went ashore to address the thousands of visitors to the exposition.[52] The naval fleet would, for the following six months, "spend as much time as possible there at anchor off Sewell's Point in Hampton Roads," in an effort to ensure the "exposition's naval success." (Bogle, 28) Roosevelt returned less than two months later on June 10, 1907, when another naval review was held in the same waters.[53] The showcasing of naval might to the American people and the world remained a focal point for the duration of the exposition. But the exposition was only a brief glimpse - a mere foundation - for the Atlantic Fleet's next set of orders from the Commander-In-Chief.

A month after his second naval review at the Jamestown Exposition, Roosevelt "leaked news on 1 July 1907 to trusted reporters." (Bogle, 29) As popular opinion soared and as the plan came together, Roosevelt realized that a circumnavigation voyage could provide both Americans and foreigners with a better understanding of the United States Navy and more importantly, its high level of efficiency. After additional months of planning and coordination, the

---

[52] Interestingly Roosevelt, who usually verbally advocated for the importance of the building and maintaining of the United States Navy, made no mention of the naval fleet or the U.S. Navy, according to the reports of his speech to the audience. The fleet at anchor in the background coupled with a military parade of United States Army soldiers and Navy sailors on the opening day, spoke volumes in and of it self. (*NYT*, 27APR1907)
[53] According to Bogle, during the second presidential review Roosevelt received a "1,806-gun salute before presiding over another military parade followed by a rousing all-American naval review." (Bogle, 28)

United States Navy received their orders for a global voyage. As a result, the order became one of the most recognizable achievements of Roosevelt's presidential naval actions. The showcase of American naval prowess when he launched the Atlantic Fleet on a circumnavigation of the world provided a visual and concrete example of Roosevelt's concept of "Walk softly and carry a big stick." It would become an integral part of the foundation of his foreign and military policies. He "first explained what the proverb meant at the Minnesota State Fair on September 2, 1901, when he was vice-president" and the United States Navy would be the most visible display of the policy during his administration. (Gable, 37) In 1907, as the United States Navy increased, he sent the Atlantic Fleet underway to show the world the efficiency and might that was possessed by the United States Government.

Statue of Capt. John Smith at Jamestown, Virginia. Author's collection.

The decision to send the Atlantic Fleet on its historic voyage around the world was based on several concerns. Part of the reason for the voyage was to dispel concerns of Japanese naval growth that was fueled by the "quick flow of Japanese labor to California," and "disturbing regulations" against the immigrants by the San Francisco School Board. (Reckner, 17) These aspects provided a breeding ground for concern by Americans who, in large part "viewed Japan as a distinct military threat to the usually defenseless West Coast and Hawaii." (Reckner, 17) In addition to the domestic concerns regarding the Japanese, much stress was placed on the might of the Japanese naval prowess due in large part to its victories over the Russians during the Russo-Japanese War. Roosevelt had war plans reviewed by the United States Army and Navy during this time frame, in case the reality of the threat posed imminent action, but the need did not arise. Upon further review of the entire time frame, though the Japan situation was a vital aspect to the launching of the Great White Fleet, it was not the single reason. In reality however, "the Navy's preoccupation with the defense implications of the 'war scare' of 1907 was quite short lived, a brief distraction from the traditional concentration on events in the Caribbean and Europe." (Reckner, 17) Nonetheless, according to historian James R. Reckner, "the voyage of the Great White Fleet…has taken its place in the annals of U.S. naval history as the single most significant American naval event of the Roosevelt administration." (Reckner, 17)[54]

On December 16, 1907, the Atlantic Fleet set sail from Hampton Roads, Virginia. The fleet of vessels consisted of four battleship squadrons and their

---

[54] Reckner points out that though the voyage was a success, "on the negative side, the world cruise graphically re-emphasized the critical shortage of supporting infrastructure on the Pacific coast, in Hawaii, Guam, and the Philippines, and the equally critical shortage of mission-designed fleet colliers and American-flag merchant ships to support the fleet. The General Board of the Navy continued to develop plans for use in the event of war with Japan. Nonetheless, the most significant conclusion drawn from the cruise was that until adequate support facilities were in place, the United States was unprepared for the battleship fleet to conduct extended combat operations in the Pacific." (Reckner, 25)

escorts. All of their hulls were painted white and adorning their bows was gilded scrollwork with red, white and blue highlights. The fleet showed to the world that the United States Navy could operate on a global scale.

For fourteen months, from December 16, 1907 to February 22, 1909, the Atlantic Fleet, later referred to as the "Great White Fleet" sailed over 43,000 miles, circumnavigating the globe. While reports of the Navy's adventures were published in myriad papers across the land for the public to follow the voyage, Roosevelt continued to vocalize and demand a "Hard-Hitting Navy." (*NYT*, 23JUL1908) One of the most prolific speeches made during this time frame was an address to the Naval War College in Newport, Rhode Island – one of his frequent stops during his career.

Roosevelt once again reiterated the need for a naval force that could efficiently and effectively be leverage in the war for peace:

> *"No fight was ever won yet except by hitting, and the one unforgivable offense in any man is to hit soft. When this Nation does have to go to war, such war will only be excusable if the Nation intends to hammer its opponent until the opponent quits fighting. The Monroe Doctrine, unbacked by the navy, is an empty boast, and there exist but few more contemptible characters, individual or National, then the man or nation who boasts and when the boast is challenged fails to make good. It is our undoubted right to say what people, what persons, shall come to this country to live, to work, and to become citizens. It is absolutely necessary that, if we claim ourselves the right to choose who shall come here, we shall be in trim to uphold that right if any power challenges it. The voyage of the sixteen battleships around South America, through the Strait of Magellan, from Hampton Roads to Puget Sound – that was the instructive object lesson that had ever been afforded as to the reality of the Monroe Doctrine."[55] (NYT, 23JUL1908)*

---

[55] Roosevelt actually spoke to two different audiences. The first address was provided to military officers, the public and the press. The second address was made to the military officers only. (*NYT*, 23JUL1908)

The cruise's first leg was to San Francisco, California. Along the way, the fleet traveled to Trinidad, Rio de Janeiro, Puna Arenas, Collan, Peru, Magdalena Bay, Mexico, and arrived in San Francisco after a total of 14, 556 miles. After roughly a month stay, the fleet left port and traveled to Honolulu, Hawaii, Auckland, New Zealand, Sydney, Melbourne, and Albay, Australia, Manila, Philippines, Yokohama, Japan, and finished the second leg at Manila for a total of 16,336 miles. The second squadron had headed to Amoy, China. The last leg of the cruise took the fleet from Manila in the Philippines to Colombo, Ceylon, Suez, Egypt, and Gibraltar, finally arriving in Hampton Roads, Virginia after traveling over 12,445 miles on the last leg.

From the deck of the Presidential yacht *Mayflower*, Roosevelt waved the fleet as they had left and now, after their historic cruise, he once again waved to them as they entered their home waters. Under a twenty-one gun salute, he cheered the 14,000 sailors with "enthusiastic waves." Two weeks later, Roosevelt would turn over control of the White House, the presidency, and the United States Navy, to his successor, William Howard Taft.

The around the world cruise of the Atlantic Fleet had various results, both diplomatically and militarily. As pointed out by Navy Journalist second class, Mike McKinley, in his article, *The Cruise of the Great White Fleet*, the "cruise satisfied our country's desire to be recognized as a world power," and that the relations "with the countries visited were improved or initially established in a positive way." (McKinley, 14) The visit to Yokohama, Japan for example, provided "the main thrust behind the Root-Takahira Agreement." (McKinley, 14) In addition, an "Open Door" policy in regards to China would also be maintained by both the United States and Japan.

The United States Navy learned much from the cruise and though the fleet had left under a cloud of "detractors," over the fourteen months, "no serious repair of maintenance problems; there were no break downs or serious accidents." (McKinley, 14) Though no major incidents occurred, "the voyage brought to light various technical defects in ship design." (McKinley, 14) During heavy weather it was determined that there was "a need for greater size and displacement of ships; shipboard habitability wasn't adequate and ventilation ad to be improved; hull casement shutters couldn't keep the water out in rough seas; rapid-fire guns placed close to the waterline could not be used effectively since spray and water shipping into the gunports were distracting to the crews; and lofty upperworks of the ships found to be comfortable for peacetime conditions but would be "shell explodes" during wartime." (McKinley, 14)

Also during the cruise, "the old-style military masts" and "fighting tops" were replaced with "new cage masts with fire-control tops; top heavy bridges and charthouses were removed and replaced by open bridges; light-weight torpedo-defense guns gave way to more powerful pieces; and new fire-control gear was fitted out on the ships." (McKinley, 14) Last, but not least, Rear Admiral Charles S. Sperry, the Commanding Officer of the ships of the Atlantic Fleet during the second and last leg of the cruise, "recommended that the ships of the Navy should have their coloration changed from white to gray." (McKinley, 15) The cruise of the "Great White Fleet" was officially over and the United States Navy and its mission would never be the same again.

Roosevelt addressing sailors upon their return. Courtesy U.S. Navy.

Upon the triumphant return of the fleet, Roosevelt explained to the Navy sailors and officers that "other nations may do what you have done, but they'll have to follow you." As Roosevelt left office in 1909, the legacy of this administration, especially in regards to the overall expansion of the United States to second only behind the Royal Navy, heralded in the attitude and direction of the government's general response to foreign policy and naval strength and preparedness for the next century.[56] Historians and critics question Roosevelt's policies, and Robert William Love, in an essay titled, *TR's Big Stick: Roosevelt and the Navy 1901-1909*, states that "Roosevelt's beliefs constituted a marvelous conflicting body of thought, and this expressed itself in no field more than naval policy and strategy."

Love argues that the origins of Roosevelt's policies are "easy to trace." In remarks made at the Naval War College in 1897, Roosevelt stated that "the American people must either build and maintain an adequate Navy or else make up their minds definitely to accept a secondary position in international affairs, not merely political, but in commercial matters." (Love, 319) Subsequently, Love explains that when Roosevelt took office, "battleships were the standard of naval strength; that is, the number of first-class battleships a nation possessed in its fleet – almost regardless of their overseas obligations, interest, bases, or the number of lesser vessels it deployed such as cruisers, destroyers, torpedo boats, fleet train, tenders, colliers, or transports – reflected relative naval power when compared with the battle fleets of the other maritime powers." (Love, 319)

---

[56] In the late days of his administration, Roosevelt passed an order that upset the cadre of U.S. Marines. In November 1908, he ordered the U.S. Marines, then stationed aboard naval vessels, to be stationed ashore in an effort to provide the ability to better distribute throughout the fleet's bases so that they could be mustered to points of interest in a more timely fashion. In addition, the expense of keeping the men at sea would be greatly diminished, and providing more room for "regular sailors." (*NYT*, 13NOV1908) The unpopular act was changed in one of Roosevelt's last acts as President when he signed the Army and Navy appropriation bills in early March 1904. The "latter bill contained the provision designed to restore the marines to the ships of the navy" which he had previously ordered. (*NYT*, 4MAR1909)

Therefore, as he continues, the "result was that Roosevelt himself gauged the success of his naval policy on the strength of the battle line." (Love, 319)

The problem as Love points out was that Roosevelt was not always clear in his thinking and that "few pre-World War 1 administrations laid out a complete, long-term naval shipbuilding program, and Roosevelt and his secretaries of the Navy more often than not simply deferred to Congress or the bureau chiefs when it came to deciding the number of lesser warships and auxiliaries to be built." (Love, 319-320) Between 1898 and 1900, Congress had approved eight battleships, but the expansion policy ended and a replacement policy became the new policy, but "either TR dramatically reversed this short-term, one-year trend, or breathed new life into McKinley's earlier expansion policy." (Love, 320) Between 1901 and 1905, Congress authorized ten first-class battleships and increased naval expenditures from roughly eighty-five million to about one-hundred and twenty million dollars. The replacement policy was revised as Roosevelt dealt with the Russo-Japanese War and its naval implications, and the splashing of the British dreadnaught. Love questions whether or not Roosevelt's expansion of the fleet, including four dreadnaught type battleships in 1908-1909, was "the result of consistent policy articulated from the top, or a continuation of the general expansionist 'drift' of the Cleveland-McKinley Years?" (Love, 320)

Love points out repeatedly in his article that Roosevelt's choices for Secretary of the Navy undermined the effectiveness of the administration's policies because the secretaries "often presented Congress with a picture of confusion and uncertainly." (Love, 322) All of the secretaries, William H. Moody, Paul Morton, Charles Joseph Bonaparte, Victor Metcalf, Truman Newbury, with exception of John D. Long, supported the expansion policy, but none of were in the post long enough to "put his own print on American naval policy." (Love, 320) As Love eloquently stated, "many of them could neither articulate nor defend the administration's naval policy." (Love, 320) Could this have been the result of an unclear policy from Roosevelt?

The efficiencies of the secretaries were sometimes a mirror of Roosevelt's own wavering actions in regards to his naval policy. For example, after Roosevelt asked for Congress in December 1901 to provide funds "for new battleship construction," he stated that his goal was merely to have a navy of "adequate size to defend the nation and uphold the Monroe Doctrine." (Love, 323) But when Secretary Moody was pushed for what the goal of the administration was and how many vessels would constitute an "adequate fleet," the answer was vague. From 1901 to 1904, Roosevelt asked for only one 16,000 ton battleship, even though the General Board had recommended three. During the election year of 1904, Roosevelt "announced a plan to maintain the fleet at existing levels" and confided to General Leonard Wood in March 1905 that the naval fleet which as he stated, "put us a good second to France and about on par with Germany." (Love, 324-325) Though later that year, Roosevelt stated that the "authorized twenty-eight battleships and twenty armored cruisers was enough and asked for a 'replacement policy' based on an average of one battleship that year and each year thereafter." (Love, 325) Congress still went forward by authorizing the "construction of two more 16,000 ton battleships." (Love, 325)

But this change from expansion to replacement changed as overseas incidents and tensions arose. By early 1907, Roosevelt had once again leaned on Congress for four battleships, but they answered by approving only two for the remainder of his second term. Roosevelt would stress the importance of a large and powerful fleet, but his naval policy, as pointed by Love and various other historians, is one that causes many to ponder the "enduring riddle about his naval policy." (Love, 326-327) Love concludes in his essay with the concept that overall, "naval policy is less the product of presidential or military planning – or military guidance-than of an interplay of personalities, public opinion, partisan politics, and overseas events." (Love, 327)

As Roosevelt left office and with the Great White Fleet in home waters, the United States Navy was at is technological zenith. In an era of huge battleships and massive fleets, under Roosevelt's leadership, though considered by some as a riddle, his overall plan for the United States Navy had been achieved. The nation's ability to "walk softly and carry a big stick," utilizing the United States Navy, her men, and her fleet, had been accomplished. In addition, though his policies shifted from replacement to expansion on several occasions, it is paramount to remember two major aspects. First, some of his shifts can be correlated to growing tensions in various parts of the world. In addition, to the foundation of a legacy that pushed the United States Navy from number five to number two in the World in the capacity of less than eight years. Wavering or not, the growth of the United States Navy, under the support and leadership of Roosevelt, can not be underestimated.

Chapter 13 - East meets West

Theodore Roosevelt had shed his Assistant Secretary of the Navy position to don a custom made Brooks Brothers uniform of the American Volunteer Group that would later be referred to as the "Rough Riders." The action of the Spanish-American War, fueled by the infamous *U.S.S. Maine* explosion, was the perfect situation in which Roosevelt could excel.

The war quickly became a two front war and this reality quickly stressed the importance of the United States Navy in relation to the geography of Latin America. When the conflict began, the battles would take place in two "widely separated areas – Cuba in the Caribbean and the Philippine Islands in the Pacific," as pointed out by Edward F. Dolan in *Panama and the United States, Their Canal, Their Stormy Years*, thus indicating the need for quick response from both the Pacific and Atlantic Oceans. (Dolan, 61)

The two fronts thrust a major issue to the forefront of both offensive and defensive strategy for the United States. How would the United States Government, and more importantly, the United States Navy best defend its possessions in the Atlantic and Pacific theaters of operation? This question was intensified even more when after the war, America garnered the Philippine Islands and Guam with an unclear ability to protect them as efficiently and effectively as might be needed in the future. Dolan provided an example to illustrate this point by stating that "at the height of the war, the battleship *Oregon* was called to Cuba. But the ship was docked in Seattle and it had to make a wild dash of 13,000 miles (20,920 km) around South America to reach the Caribbean." (Dolan, 61)

By 1899, the United States Government had formed a special commission with the charge of determining the best location for a canal to be built. To further the reality of the project, "Congress began discussing a bill that would allocate $180 million for the digging of a Nicaraguan canal." (Dolan, 61) But the French Government had already begun a canal project in the 1870's. In an effort to revive its global prestige after its loss to the Germans in the Franco-Prussian War of 1870-1871, the French "decided to take and complete one of history's most challenging engineering projects – the linking of the world's two greatest oceans." (Dolan, 53) After reviewing both Panama and Nicaraguan geography, France chose Panama and negotiated with Columbia for permission. The French estimated that cost of the canal at "1,174 million francs (at the time, the equivalent of $214 million)." But the millions of francs would not come from the government coffers, but rather from private investors "on the promise that they would profit from the fees to be charged to ships using the passage." (Dolan, 54) In 1879, Ferdinand de Lesseps, famed Frenchman who had led the completion of the Suez Canal, was chosen president of the new company.

In 1881, the French began the project, even though there was major dissension within the company as many of the engineers disagreed with Lessep's planned route. But Culebra Hill, a 300 foot high roadblock soon was the least of the developer's worries. "The French quickly learned that Panama was one of the world's unhealthiest places." (Dolan, 56) Yellow fever and malaria soon began to take a human toll on the workers and the diseases, "killed more than 22,000 of the Indians, Jamaicans, Chinese, and whites who worked on the canal." (Dolan, 56)

By 1887 the company had "run out of money and was unable to raise additional funds." (Dolan, 59) The French abandoned the waterway project even though they "had managed to finish two-fifths of the waterway." (Dolan, 59) Though the French had retreated from the project, the United States was interested. After the Spanish-American War, the French still had claim to the canal project and though Lessep's company was defunct, a new French company was formed. The new company decided to make the United States an offer that it would "sell its Panamanian holdings, including its equipment and the stretch of the canal that had already been dug." (Dolan, 62) The offer was made to the United States for a sum of over $100 million dollars.

The United States Government scoffed at the offer and countered the French company by stating that the United States Government "would take over the holdings for a much smaller amount: $40 million. It would also, however, only after it had received permission from Columbia to dig in Panama." (Dolan, 62) The French firm believed the counter offer to be an insult, but when they realized that the United States was the only interested party, they decided that any offer was better then no offer. Before monies exchanged hands however, "Washington undertook two steps – one with Great Britain and one with Columbia."

A treaty with Britain, the Clayton-Bulwer Treaty, provided that if either country proceeded with a canal project that both the U.S. and British governments would "act together in its development and construction." (Dolan, 52) In addition, another significant proviso was that both countries agreed to "keep the canal neutral in the event of war and leave it open to their ships." (Dolan, 52) But as the eventuality of the United States' efforts to complete the project became more realistic, many Americans vocalized their dissatisfaction stating that the treaty was a violation of the Monroe Doctrine.

But Britain was not in steadfast to the provisions of the treaty and relinquished their rights because if they had wanted to stand by the treaty, they would have had to provide both financial and manpower assistance to the project. Due to their involvement in the Boer War in South Africa, "Britain had neither to spare at the time." (Dolan, 63) Therefore in 1901, a new treaty was established. The Hay-Pauncefote Treaty was set which "called for Great Britain to give the United States the right to act independently in the development of an Atlantic-Pacific waterway." (Dolan, 63) The additional provisions of the treaty were that the "Britain agreed that the United States would close the canal to British shipping if it so desired in times of war," and that the United States would "keep the canal open to the shipping of all nations in times of peace and to charge an equal fee to all ships using the water passage." (Dolan, 63) One political obstacle had been overcome, but another, Columbia, remained unresolved.

Columbia represented the next hurtle for the United States Government's plan for the canal. John Hay, U.S. Secretary of State under President Roosevelt "opened negotiations with the Columbian government," with the result of the meetings being the Hay-Herran Treaty. (Dolan, 63) The treaty "which granted to the United States a strip of land 6 miles (9.6 km) wide along the general route laid out by de Lesseps." (Dolan, 63) In addition, the United States was permitted the ability to "administer and police" this strip of land around the canal. Lastly, the United States agreed to pay Columbia $10 million dollars and after 9 years from the date of completion, the United States would pay an annual fee of $250,000.

The United States Congress approved the treaty in March of 1903, but the Columbian Congress demanded more money. The Panamanians, who would benefit most from the project, reacted with a revolution. Columbia, in an effort to squash the rebellion sent five hundred troops to Panama. Though it was rumored that the United States was in support of the Panamanian uprising it was not until, "President Roosevelt ordered U.S. warships to Panama City and sent the gunboat *Nashville*, with a detachment of Marines onboard, to Colon," had action replaced rumor. (Dolan, 65)

Utilizing the Bidlack Treaty, which stated free passage across Panama would not be endangered by any fighting, the Captain of the *U.S.S. Nashville* prevented the Columbian troops, with the exception of the officers, to cross the Isthmus. "Under the guise of protecting its rights of free passage, the United States kept the Columbian troops in Colon, and thus ensured the success of the rebellion." (Dolan, 65) Without bloodshed, the rebellion was successful and on November 3, 1903, Panama became an independent country. By November 6, 1903, the United States formally recognized it as such.

By November 18, 1903, the Hay-Bunau-Varilla Treaty was signed, the forty million dollar payment was made to the French company, and permission was granted by the Panamanian representative, Philippe Bunau-Varilla which opened the way for the canal to be constructed. The United States Congress ratified the treaty in 1904. The canal and access between the two great oceans, the Atlantic and the Pacific, was on its way. Dolon points out that "in some ways, the Varilla Treaty was identical to the Hay-Herran Treaty," but there were some significant differences. Monies would instead be paid to the new Panamanian Government, the Panama Canal Zone was extended to five miles on each side of the canal, and the area would be under complete United States control. (Dolan, 69)

Construction began on the Canal in May of 1904 and would take ten years to complete. The total cost of the project was "almost $367 million" dollars. (Dolan, 71) An intricate and efficient system of locks, man-made locks, and dams, provided a forty mile waterway that linked the two oceans for the first time. The ability to send United States Naval warships, gunboats, supplies and troops was finally available.

U.S. submarines passing through the Gatun Locks of the Canal. Author's collection.

Roosevelt's hand in the Panama Canal project can not be underestimated. During multiple speeches Roosevelt made his position well known to those in government office and the public. On June 21st and 22nd of 1905, Roosevelt completed three college commencement exercises, including one where he received an honorary degree of Doctor of Letters. During the last address, he reiterated his position to the graduates regarding the Monroe Doctrine, the Panama Canal, and the United States Navy. "Therefore see to it that the navy is built up and kept to the highest point of efficiency...I believe in the Monroe Doctrine; I believe in the builder and maintaining of the Panama Canal...keep on building and maintaining the United Stats Navy, or quit trying to be a big Nation. Do one or the other." (*NYT*, 23JUN1905) Roosevelt elected to have the Canal built by the government and his continued support both diplomatically and by the use of the United States Navy to help Panama establish its independence was vital to the completion of the project.[57] The lasting effects of the canal project under the presidential leadership of Roosevelt though marred throughout the canal's history by varying degrees of Latin American interactions until the establishment of the Good Neighbor Policy, is best summarized by Dolan in regards to the use of the Canal in a later world-wide conflict.

> *"During World War II, the canal provided a speedy Atlantic-Pacific service for warships, troopships, freighters carrying military hardware and goods. Because of this service, the canal enabled the United States to fight a war in two oceans with an efficiency that would have been otherwise impossible." (Dolan, 113)*

---

[57] Roosevelt traveled to the Panama Canal Project in 1906 and marked "the first trip abroad by a U.S. President in office," according to Edmund Morris. The "colossal excavations there moved him to Shakespearean hyperbole. 'It shall be in future enough to say of any man he was connected with digging the Panama Canal' to confer the patent of nobility on that man,' Roosevelt told his sweating engineers. (Morris, xv)

Chapter 14 - The Lasting Legacy

The legacy of Roosevelt was not relegated to presidential reviews, fleet maneuvers, mid-day meals with enlisted personnel, and a submarine voyage beneath the waves of the Long Island Sound.[58] During the two administrations as Commander in Chief, he provided an open sea of possibilities to the waterborne branch of the armed services. The most prolific example of his support was chiefly mirrored in his West African proverb of "Speak softly and carry a big stick, you will go far." This proverb, not only exemplified his attitude regarding the United States Navy, but more effectively, represented most of his presidential duties and actions.

Roosevelt had been advocating the necessity for a strong navy since the publication of his history of the naval war of 1812 and during his brief tenure as the Assistant Secretary of the Navy. Once president in 1901, Roosevelt had the ability and power to effectively transform the Navy from its fifth world-place ranking, into a superior fighting force. Upon his leaving office in 1909, the United States Navy ranked second in the World only to the British Navy. According to the Department of the Navy's Naval Historical Center, the United States Navy had in December 1898 the following vessels in her fleet:

6 battleships
18 cruisers
14 monitors
0 destroyers
12 torpedo boats
34 steel gunboats
30 auxiliaries
16 screw steamers

---

[58] Roosevelt's support and legacy is also visible as it reflected change in other countries and their leaders. The German Navy for example, which for some time "regarded submarines as useless toys…changed its opinion and persuaded the Reichstag to appropriate 5,000,000 marks for the construction of submarines." (*NYT*, 23MAY1906) Emperor William in late May of 1906 inspected one of Simon Lake's crafts in Kiel and many reporters believed that they would not be surprised if "he followed President Roosevelt's example and made a descent in one of them." (*NYT*, 23MAY1906)

4 screw sloops
1 sailing ship
25 gunboats

With a total of 160 active vessels. (114 steel, 46 old navy)

These numbers radically changed by the second year of President Roosevelt's administration. In addition to an overall increase of vessels, several additional types of vessels or crafts were added as well. As of December 1903 the United States Navy Fleet consisted of:

11 battleships
19 cruisers
6 monitors
16 destroyers
27 torpedo boats
8 submarines
29 steel gunboats
26 auxiliaries
9 screw steamers
2 screw sloops
22 gunboats

With a total of 175 vessels. (142 steel, 33 old navy)

By the end of Roosevelt's second presidential administration, the true reflection of his push for a strong navy became apparent. As of December 1909 the United States Naval fleet consisted of:

25 battleships
27 cruisers
2 monitors
20 destroyers
33 torpedo boats
16 submarines
19 steel gunboats
29 auxiliaries
16 gunboats

With a total of 187 vessels.

The most significant change during his time at the helm was the increase of not only the total number of vessels in the United States Naval fleet, but also the size of the vessels added to the fleet. Battleships, which number only six in 1898 reached 25, and destroyers, which did not exist in the fleet in 1898, were 20 deep by 1909. Submarines, which totaled eight in active service in 1903 doubled in six years to 16.

As it became apparent that the world was marching into a global conflict, both on land and at sea, Roosevelt initially assailed getting involved. However, as time went on and the atrocities of the war became all too hard to ignore, Roosevelt championed becoming a major support of the ideals of the allied forces. In addition to attempting to gain a military commission to lead a rough riding similar troop into battle, Roosevelt wrote articles advancing his viewpoints on his contemporaries in the White House and his opinions regarding the war-effort and armed services. In an article written by Roosevelt that was published on November 22, 1914 in the *New York Times* and other newspapers, he outlined "The Navy as a Peacemaker."[59]

Outlining his stance with his usual vigor, Roosevelt explained that the United States Navy was the key to our defense.

> *"The right arm of the nation must be its navy. Our navy is our most efficient peacemaker. In order to use the navy effectively we should clearly define to ourselves the policy we intend to follow and the limits over which we expect our power to extend. Our own coasts, Alaska, Hawaii, and the Panama Canal and its approaches should represent the sphere in which we should expect to be able singlehanded [sp] to meet and master any opponent from overseas."*

Roosevelt continued by outlining his dissatisfaction with the then current status of the administration of the Navy Department, and the United States government in general.

---

[59] His article, Navy as a Peacemaker, was part of a series of articles published in a variety of newspapers around the country. Navy as a Peacemaker was number eight in the series.

"During the last twenty months, ever since Secretary Meyer left the Navy Department, there has been in our navy a great falling off relatively to other nations. It was quite impossible to avoid this while our national affairs were handled has they have recently been handled. The President who intrusts [sp] the Department of State and the Navy to gentlemen like Messrs. Bryan and Daniels deliberately invites disaster in the event of serious complications with a formidable foreign opponent."

To illustrate his point more effectively, Roosevelt turned to his knowledge of history.

"It has been said that the United States never learns by experience but only by disaster. Such method of education may at times prove costly. The slothful or shortsighted citizens who are now misled by the cries of the ultra-pacifists would do well to remember events connected with the outbreak of the war with Spain."

In closing Roosevelt echoed the importance of the "only really useful defensive is the offensive" by explaining that:

"The navy of the United States is the right arm of the United States and is emphatically the Peacemaker. Woe to our country if we permit that right arm to become palsied or even to become flabby and inefficient."

Though Roosevelt advocated for continued building of the naval fleet after his leaving office, the additions to the fleet dwindled in the early teens. Much of Roosevelt's momentum had been lost as he left the halls of government. The lack of building would be addressed only when the growing threat of German submarine warfare during the First World War reared its ugly periscope. In a major push, the United States Navy's fleet expanded to an amazing 774 vessels by November 11, 1918. Though peace treaties and other circumstances would force a dwindling of the war-time numbers dramatically, the United States Navy's next largest fleet would come, on the crest of the Second World War. By the end of the war, August 14, 1945, when a tally was taken, the United States

Naval fleet had reached a fleet of 6,768 vessels – the zenith of the United States Navy.[60]

But more important than the increase of the fleet, was the tone that Roosevelt had set for the United States Navy. A few years after his passing, the Navy League proposed that October 27th of each year be declared Navy Day. The celebration, which first took place in 1922, commemorates and celebrates the United States Navy and the anniversary of Roosevelt's birthday. Navy Day is a true honor bestowed to one of the Navy's largest and most vocal supporters.[61] Interestingly, as pointed out by Edward J. Renehan, Jr., the date of October 27th is also the anniversary of a "1775 report issued by a special committee of the Continental Congress favoring the purchase of merchant ships as the foundation of an American Navy. Isn't it interesting that Theodore Roosevelt and the United States Navy should share the same birthday? How big a coincidence can that be? Or is it no coincidence at all?" (Theodore Roosevelt Association)

In addition to the yearly honor of Navy Day, during the post-World War II era the United States Navy launched a Fleet Ballistic Missile Submarine of the *George Washington-class*, bearing the Roosevelt name. The initial contract was awarded on March 13, 1958 and the *U.S.S. Theodore Roosevelt* began its construction on "components initially assembled for the *Skipjack-class* nuclear attack submarine *Scamp* (SSN-588)" at Mare Island, California. (DANFS) She was launched on October 3, 1959 and was originally outfitted with Polaris (A-1)

---

[60] The fleet as of June 30, 1950 would only be 634 total vessels. The numbers of course increased during times of conflicts including Korea and Vietnam. The next major downsizing would take place in 1968-69 when the United States Navy began decommissioning many World War II-era ships.

[61] In an October 28, 1922 *New York Times* article titled *Navy and Roosevelt Honored in Capital*, the reporter states that "the spirit of Theodore Roosevelt walked abroad in Washington today. Though formal celebration of his birthday was claimed by the navy for its own-and there is no one who would challenge the navy's right to revel in memories of Roosevelt, to pay gladly the debt of gratitude it owes to him – everywhere there ran a curious undercurrent of talk among men that bore witness to the place the dead President had made for himself in American hearts." In addition, a wreath was placed on Roosevelt's tomb at Oyster Bay – a tradition that continues to today. (*NYT*, 28OCT1922)

missiles, providing the submarine with the ability to fight the cold war from the deep recesses of the abyss.[62] *U.S.S. Theodore Roosevelt* was commissioned in the United States Navy on February 13, 1961, with Mrs. Alice Roosevelt, acting as the submarine's sponsor.

U.S.S. Roosevelt model at the Mariner's Museum. Author's collection.

The *U.S.S. Theodore Roosevelt* was a three hundred and eighty two foot long submarine with a thirty-three foot beam and a draft of twenty-nine feet. Her total crew consisted of 139 officers and enlisted personnel. The submarine received orders for the east coast and on March 7, "she became the first ballistic missile submarine (FBM) to transit the Panama Canal." (DANFS) After her arrival off of Cape Canaveral, Florida, the *U.S.S. Theodore Roosevelt*

---

[62] The *George Washington* Class comprised of five submarines – *Abraham Lincoln, Robert E. Lee, Theodore Roosevelt, Patrick Henry*, and George *Washington*. The original armament of Polaris (A-1) missiles was "replaced with Polaris (A-3) missiles at General Dynamics, Groton...between 6-10-64 and 6-3-67. The refit included overhaul, refueling and replacement of the compress-air missile ejection system with a gas-steam ejection system." (Morison, 43)

successfully fired one of her Polaris missiles, completed her training cruise and then headed to the naval submarine base at Groton, Connecticut. After a few month overhaul and repairs at Groton, she headed south to prepare for her first deterrent patrol. From 1961 to 1978, the *U.S.S. Theodore Roosevelt* would complete forty three patrols.[63] She was decommissioned in 1981, but the legacy would continue in the form of a nuclear aircraft carrier.

After the decommissioning of the submarine, a new vessel was launched bearing Roosevelt's name. On October 25, 1986, the United States Navy commissioned *CVN 71 Theodore Roosevelt*. The nuclear powered aircraft carrier's construction contract was awarded to the Newport News Shipbuilding Company on September 30, 1980 and her keel was laid down a year and thirty one days later on October 31, 1981. She was launched on Navy Day, 1984 and was commissioned two years later on October 25, 1986. The *Nimitz-class* vessel is approximately ninety-seven thousand tons in displacement and is over one thousand feet long with a beam overall at two hundred and fifty-two feet. Her maximum navigational draft is thirty-seven feet and she is propelled through the water by two Westinghouse A4W nuclear reactors. The nuclear propulsion system allows for her endurance to only be limited by her food stores and she can cruise at thirty plus knots. A virtual floating city, the aircraft carrier has a crew complement of thirty-two hundred officers and enlisted company with an attached air wing of close to twenty-five hundred. After her testing and shakedown cruises and exercises, the *U.S.S. Theodore Roosevelt* entered service with the Atlantic Fleet and in December of 1990, she cruised for support of Operation Desert Shield. The fighter wing would be responsible for over four thousand combat sorties and were responsible for dropping more than four million pounds of ordinance during the conflict. After her service and support of Operation Desert Shield, she was active in Operation Provide Comfort, Operation

---

[63] The *U.S.S. Theodore Roosevelt* sailed from the Fleet Ballistic Missile base at Holy Loch, Scotland for the majority of her time in service. After a complete overhaul in 1974, she was reassigned to the Pacific Fleet, home-ported in Pearl Harbor Hawaii. (DANFS)

Deny Flight, Operation Southern Watch, NATO's Operation Allied Force, and most recently Operations Enduring Freedom and Operation Iraqi Freedom. During her twenty-two years of service in the United States Navy, the *U.S.S. Theodore Roosevelt* has been a rugged performer during both peacetime and wartime operations. With her nickname *T.R.* and her call sign *Big Stick*, her command and crew effectively and affectionately honor and continue the proud legacy of their ship's namesake in their day to day operations in home waters or abroad.[64]

U.S.S. Theodore Roosevelt underway. Courtesy U.S. Navy.

As time has passed on, the legacy of Theodore Roosevelt still resonates throughout the fleet and for that matter, the world. With ships such as *the U.S.S. Theodore Roosevelt* which is not only a ship, but also a carrier group, honoring the name of the father of the modern U.S. Navy, Roosevelt's legacy as a champion proponent of the naval services continues as the United States sails into harm's way to carry the big stick of diplomacy.

---

[64] Many of the ship's patches are adorned with representations of Theodore Roosevelt.

Chapter 15 – Conclusion

"Whoever commands the sea,
commands the trade;
whosoever commands the trade of the world,
commands the riches of the world,
and consequently the world itself."

Sir Walter Raleigh, Circa 1610

President Theodore Roosevelt passed away in his sleep on January 6, 1919 at his home, Sagamore Hill, in Oyster Bay, New York. He was sixty years of age. Two years earlier, he had requested an approval from President Woodrow Wilson to "raise a company similar to the Rough Riders in 1898 and take it to France." (Auchincloss, 132) Roosevelt, age fifty-eight, was at the time of his meeting with the President, suffering from rheumatism, was overweight, and had a detached retina injury from his years as President. His request was denied. Roosevelt continued his vigilance in fighting Washington and more especially President Woodrow Wilson. "Unable to fight against the Germans, TR continued to wage his own private war against the Wilson administration at home." (Collier, 205) The war, in which he was unable to fight personally, remained a constant vigil that Roosevelt spearheaded, both privately, and in public.[65] Weeks

---

[65] Regarding his outspoken devotion for the war effort of a personal nature – "One night during a patriotic rally at Madison Square Garden he had just begun to speak when a heckler shouted, 'What have you done for the war effort?' Taken aback for a moment, TR paused, blinked nearsightedly out into the darkness before replying in a voice breaking with emotion: 'What am I doing for my country in this war? I have sent my four boys, for each of whose lives I care a thousand more than I care for my own, if you can understand that…" (Collier, 204) The Roosevelt's would lose one of their sons during the war, Quentin. A pilot during the war, Quentin was shot down during a dogfight with German fighter planes in July of 1918. Quentin was hit "squarely in the forehead by a machine gun shell," and was buried with full military honors by the Germans. (Collier, 232) The loss of Quentin was a tremendous blow to Theodore Roosevelt and according to friends and family; it was a loss from which he never truly recovered. Theodore Roosevelt Jr., Brigadier General in the United States Army landed with his troops on Utah Beach, during the D-Day invasion of Normandy during World War Two. Awarded the Medal of Honor for his heroism during the landings and subsequent fighting inland, Roosevelt "striding up and down the beach, cane in hand," the result of a World War One

before his passing, though he had suffered from some medical issues and had been hospitalized, continued work on a few articles, and had alluded to running for office in 1920. Roosevelt was, up until his eyes closed for the last time, a man who advocated and lived a strenuous life. Roosevelt, an American legend had passed away. Archibald, more commonly referred to as "Archie" cabled his siblings of the news in a one sentence telegram - "The old lion is dead." (Collier, 243) At the time of his passing, Vice President Thomas R. Marshall stated, "Death had to take Roosevelt sleeping, for if he had been awake, there would have been a fight." (Collier, 243)

His legacy and contributions to the both the United States and the World remain an integral part of our present day society. He left an astounding catalog of research that chronicled historical events and scientific discovery, a host of natural expanses, a solid foundation for domestic and international policies, and of course, a strong United States Navy. Roosevelt had been a champion of international affairs.

> *"To Roosevelt the aggressive diplomat, a large and efficient navy constituted a primary tool for the conduct of foreign policy. Hence he launched a program to raise the United States Navy up to a standard of efficiency and strength. He enlarged the fleet, modernized its ships, increased both its officer corps and enlisted complement, and improved efficiency through better training."* (DANFS)

In addition, Roosevelt modernized and organized the previously "scattered over the earth" fleets by formalizing the ships into three separate, but distinct fleets including, "the Atlantic Fleet (including all battleships), the Pacific Fleet, and the Asiatic Fleet." He had launched the Great White Fleet on a naval

---

injury, "urged the men forward." (Gilbert, 142) General Roosevelt succumbed to a heart attack shortly after the landings and was buried in the American National Cemetery "on the bluff of Omaha beach." His brother was "brought from elsewhere in France and reburied next to him." The Roosevelt brothers represent, "one of thirty pairs of brothers" buried in the cemetery. (Gilbert, 143)

parade that illustrated to the citizens of the World that the United States Navy would and could operate in the waters of the Caribbean or in the far reaches of foreign seas, effectively and efficiently. These are but a few of the myriad examples of how Theodore Roosevelt fought firmly for a strong and efficient naval force to carry the "big stick" of American foreign policy. It is a stick that remains held and yielded when deemed necessary. The examples also act to illustrate how Roosevelt raised the bar for the United States Navy, its enlisted men and officers, and for the future of the United States. The legacy of Theodore Roosevelt, the twenty-sixth president of the United States, has and will forever more, be a significant swath of cloth in the fabric of our history.

Roosevelt was buried in an oak casket on a hill near his home Sagamore Hill in Oyster Bay, New York. Members of the community can visit his childhood home in New York City, the summer white house – Sagamore Hill, the various national parks, and other venues. However, the *U.S.S. Plunger*, the small, cramped creation of John Holland, has become a mere footnote in the evolutionary process of the United States Navy. The *U.S.S. Plunger*, like her sister submarines, battleships and other fleet vessels, which were ultimately lost to the ravages of battle or the blazing torch of salvagers, had provided in a technological manner, the catalyst for change and for a foundation of the greatness of the United States Navy. Their contribution to the evolutionary process provided the ability for the United States Navy to expand and surpass the other navies of the World. Amalgamations of metal and steel, the ships and submarines however, were more than just vehicles of change, but rather they assisted in the gradual process of technological advances, innovation and efficiency.

Men like John Paul Jones, Chester Nimitz, John Barry, and Theodore Roosevelt fought for the United States Navy with a passionate vigor fueled by devout patriotism and knowledge of naval strategy and history. A year after October 27th was dedicated to the United States Navy an editorial appeared in the pages of the *New York Times*. It reflected, appropriately, the legacy of Theodore Roosevelt. "To the end of his days no American had a sounder judgment than THEODORE ROOSEVELT of an adequate navy, the best of ships and a personnel equal in skill to any in the world." (*NYT*, 27OCT1923) The legacy of those men, and the hundreds of thousands of men and women who have worn the United States Navy uniform in proud service to their country and world, will remain clearly visible every time a naval vessel's anchor is weighed and the mighty grey ships of the United States Navy steam into the unknown of the future.

Epilogue

In 1906, President Theodore Roosevelt was awarded the Nobel Peace Prize for his efforts in the negotiations that precipitated and allowed for the Treaty of Portsmouth – ending the Russo-Japanese War. Roosevelt was humbled by the prize and accepted only the medal and a diploma. Though he related to his son Kermit that "he would not accept as a personal gift a sum of money earned as a public figure. 'But I hated to come to the decision, because I very much wisht for the extra money to leave to all you children." (Morris, 473) Roosevelt instead donated the money to form "a foundation to establish at Washington a permanent Industrial Peace Committee." (Morris, 473)

Roosevelt's money however would not be utilized in that fashion. By 1918, with the World engrossed in the War to End all Wars, Roosevelt requested the funds returned to him from the specially created Congressional fund so that he could donate it to various organizations.[66] Roosevelt received the peace prize, the first American to ever win a Nobel Prize of any category, for his diplomatic efforts in bringing peace to a vicious war between the Russians and Japanese. His efforts had taken place, initially in the warm summer waters of Oyster Bay, Long Island, New York. Aboard the *Mayflower*, delegates from Russia and Japan met to work out their differences. During a toast to commence the ceremonies, Roosevelt stated:

> *"Gentlemen, I propose a toast to which there will be no answer...I drink to the welfare and prosperity of the sovereigns and peoples of the two great nations whose representatives have met on this ship. It is my most earnest hope and pray...that a just and lasting peace may speedily be concluded among them." (Marhoefer, 92)*

---

[66] According to Ed Renehan, Jr. in his book *The Lion's Pride*, Roosevelt "made twenty-eight different donations of various amounts. A few of the gifts included $6,900 to the Red Cross; $5,000 to Eleanor for her Y.M.C.A. project; an additional $4,000 to the YMCA National War Work Council; and $1,000 to Edith's sister, Emily Carow, a volunteer with the Italian Red Cross at Porto Maurizo, Italy." (TRA website)

It was during this same time frame – August 1905 – that Roosevelt had made his historic dive beneath the same waters aboard the *U.S.S. Plunger*. Roosevelt, a proponent for a strong navy and military was, at the same time (recognized a year later for his efforts) proposing and effectively helping to steer the warring nations toward a peaceful accord.[67] His efforts, once again, illustrate the boundless energy and amazing foresight of the father of the modern United States Navy, President Theodore Roosevelt - a true Navy man – heart and soul.

---

[67] Roosevelt was always interested in how the U.S. Navy ranked in its efficiency with other nations' naval fleets. During a talk with Dr. James Scherer, the president of Newberry College, a man who had spent many years in Japan, Dr. Scherer expressed that he was of the "opinion that, man for man, the Japanese Navy was the best in the world." (*NYT*, 24JAN1906) The comment of course struck a deep chord in President Roosevelt who retorted the comments that "in the unfortunate event of a war between America and Japan, the Americans would defeat the Japanese, ship for ship." (*NYT*, 24 JAN1906) It would be thirty-nine years before Roosevelt's opinion would be realized as fact.

Post-Script

My wife Kendall and I pushed our son's strollers along the pathways leading to Theodore Roosevelt's home, Sagamore Hill. Commonly referred to as the Summer White House, it was on these grounds that Roosevelt raised his family, experienced great triumphs, suffered great loss, enjoyed his pastimes, and ultimately passed away. As we explored the home, the third time in the previous two years, a host of interesting artifacts and reminders of Roosevelt's life are found amongst the rooms of the home. Volumes of books in his library, trophies from safaris, photographs, trinkets, and more, occupy the home. As we walked through the home, I found myself traveling to a distant time when Roosevelt walked along the floor boards, descended the stairs, and made the house his home.

It had been a little over a year since I had last visited Sagamore Hill. I had promised myself that I would not return back to its grounds until I had completed my research into Roosevelt's historic and often forgotten trip aboard the *Plunger* submarine in 1905. My research had been delayed and pushed aside for other research volumes, articles, graduate studies, and of course, work and family responsibilities. But throughout the time period, I had always found myself enamored and fascinated by Roosevelt's brief trip beneath the waves and his life-long passion and support for the U.S. Navy. After the two years of on-again-off-again research, I had finally been able to fulfill my promise. Much had changed in my life during that same timeframe. My second son Liam, who on my first trip to Sagamore Hill in 2006 was only a topic of conversation and speculation, had now celebrated his second birthday.

After our tour and after a long walk around the grounds, we got in our truck and began driving home. As we drove along the roadway, I peered at the long line of trees that separated the front lawn of the home from its previous view of Oyster Bay Harbor. As we drove onto Cove Neck Road, I pulled the truck over along the shoulder and got the boys out of their seats. In what felt like an almost solemn reflection, we peered out upon the calm August waters.

Looking out upon Oyster Bay. Author's collection.

I reflected upon Roosevelt's historic plunge beneath the waves and upon my own immersion into his naval legacy. I gazed down and watched as my two sons, the usual source of much chatter, were also looking out upon the waters, watching the sailboats, and the sun's reflection upon the water.

As I gazed at the boys, I thought of Roosevelt and imagined how he felt when he took the small launch out to meet the crew of the submarine. I wonder if he too had the vision that I and my two sons had as we looked out upon the same body of water. The future will always hold infinite possibilities, but one must be willing to open his eyes and take a look. One hundred and three years have passed since Roosevelt's historic trip aboard the submarine – but nonetheless, some things remain unchanged…thankfully.

Adam Grohman
Sagamore Hill
Oyster Bay Cove, New York
August 2008

References

The following references are listed by chapter heading.

Introduction – Syllogism & the Gray Haze of Historical Research

Nugent, Walter T.K. *Creative History – An Introduction to Historical Study*. J.B. Lippincott Company. New York, N.Y. 1967.

Parrish, Thomas. *The Submarine – A History*. Viking Penguin. New York, N.Y. 2004.

Chapter 1 - Orders and Anticipation

Hagedorn, Hermann. *The Roosevelt Family of Sagamore Hill*. The Macmillan Company. New York, N.Y. 1954.

Hutchinson, Robert. *Jane's Submarines – War Beneath the Waves from 1776 to the Present Day*. Harper Collins Publishers. 2005.

Karppi, *Walter G. Teddy Roosevelt and the Plunger*. Article. *The Freeholder: Magazine*. The Oyster Bay Historical Society. Oyster Bay, New York. Summer Edition - 2003.

Newspaper Archives – Proquest Archives. *The New York Times* – www.nytimes.com

> *The Daily Northwestern*
> August 10, 1905 - President May Take Dip, Submarine Called For.

> *The Fort Wayne Evening Sentinel*
> August 10, 1905 - President to Take Dive in Submarine

> *The New York Times*
> January 24, 1905 – Diving Boat Nearly Sank
> July 7, 1905 – French Submarine Sinks
> July 16, 1905 – Submarine Raised at Last
> August 20, 1905 – Tests of the Plunger
> August 22, 1905 – Defect in the Plunger

> *The Oakland Tribune*

August 10, 1905 – President May Dive

The Washington Post
August 13, 1905 – Lodge at Oyster Bay

Chapter 2 - Theodore Roosevelt

Blank-Reid, Cynthia. *Historic Trauma Cases – Theodore Roosevelt*. Article. *Advance For Nurses Magazine*. February 19, 2007.

Pringle, Henry F. *Theodore Roosevelt*. Harcourt, Brace & World, Inc. New York, N.Y. Second Edition. 1956. First published in 1931.

Chapter 3 - In Oyster Bay

Hagedorn, Hermann. *The Roosevelt Family of Sagamore Hill*. The Macmillan Company. New York, N.Y. 1954.

Newspaper Archives –*The New York Times* – www.nytimes.com

The New York Times
August 23, 1905 – Plunger at Oyster Bay

Chapter 4 - The Submarine

Chief of Naval Operations. Submarine Warfare Division. *The Sage of the Submarine – Early Years to the Beginning of Nuclear Power*. Article. Available online. (The article originally appeared in the September 1967 issue of *All Hands*. The text of the article was updated in 2000)

Cussler, Clive. *The Sea Hunters II*. G.P. Putnam's Sons. New York, N.Y. 2002.

Freuchen, Peter. *Peter Freuchen's Book of the Seven Seas*. Julian Messner, Inc. New York, N.Y. 1957.

Grohman, Adam M. *Beneath the Blue & Grey Waves – Sub-Marine Warfare of the American Civil War*. Ships of the Seas Series Project #2. Underwater Historical Research Society. Lulu Publishing Company. 2007.

Gunton, Michael. *Submarine's at War – A History of Undersea Warfare from the American Revolution to the Cold War*. Carroll & Graf Publishers. New York, N.Y. 2003.

Harris, Brayton. *World Submarine History Timeline – 1580-2000*. Chronological listing provided for Nova based on Harris' book The Navy Times Book of Submarines: A Political, Social and Military History. Sections 1580-1869, 1870-1914, and 1914-1945 accessed.) Available online.

Hutchinson, Robert. *Jane's Submarines – War Beneath the Waves from 1776 to the Present Day*. Harper Collins Publishers. 2005.

Office of Naval Research. Department of the Navy. *Submarines: How They Work – Archimedes' Principle*. Article. Science & Technology Focus Section. Available online.

Parrish, Thomas. *The Submarine – A History*. Viking Penguin. New York, N.Y. 2004.

Chapter 5 - A Naval Historian

Anderson, Bern. *By Sea and by River – The Naval History of the Civil War*. Da Capo Press, Inc. New York, N.Y. 1989. First edition printed 1962.

Gable, John Allen. *America's 26th President – Theodore Roosevelt – Famous American Series*. Eastern National Publishing Company. 2003.

Newspaper Archives –*The New York Times* – www.nytimes.com

> *The New York Times*
> June 5, 1882 – New Publications – Our Navy in 1812

West, Richard S. Jr. *Admirals of American Empire*. The Bobbs-Merrill Company. New York. N.Y. 1948.

Chapter 6 - Assistant Secretary of the Navy

Gable, John. Introduction to *The Naval War of 1812* – by Theodore Roosevelt. Modern Library Paperback Edition. Random House, Inc. New York, N.Y.

Morris, Edmund. *The Rise of Theodore Roosevelt*. Random House, Inc. New York, N.Y. Modern Library Paperback Edition. 2001. First edition published by Coward, McCann & Geoghegan, 1979.

Pringle, Henry F. *Theodore Roosevelt*. Harcourt, Brace & World, Inc. New York, N.Y. Second Edition. 1956. First published in 1931.

Potter, E.B. *The Naval Academy Illustrated History of the United States Navy.* Galahad Books. New York City, N.Y. 1971.

Newspaper Archives –*The New York Times* – www.nytimes.com

> *The New York Times*
> > May 13, 1897 – Navy Yard Investigation
> > July 31, 1897 – Naval Battalions Review
> > October 22, 1897 – Honor to Old Ironsides
> > December 31, 1897 – Naval Personnel Report
> > March 17, 1898 – The Navy Reorganization Bill
> > May 11, 1898 – Mr. Roosevelt's Farewell
> > May 12, 1898 – Roosevelt's Office Leaving
> > December 1, 1898 – Roosevelt on the New Navy
> > December 12, 1903 – Our Navy
> > February 4, 1904 - Long's Naval History Barred

West, Richard S. Jr. *Admirals of American Empire.* The Bobbs-Merrill Company. New York. N.Y. 1948.

Chapter 7 - Beneath the Waves

Hagedorn, Hermann. *The Roosevelt Family of Sagamore Hill.* The Macmillan Company. New York, N.Y. 1954.

Irwin, Will. *Letters to Kermit from Theodore Roosevelt – 1902-1908.* Charles Scribner's Sons. New York, New York. 1946.

Morison, Elting E. *The Letters of Theodore Roosevelt.* Volume IV – The Square Deal, 1903-1905. Harvard University Press. Cambridge, Massachusetts. 1951.

Newspaper Archives –*The New York Times* – www.nytimes.com

> *The New York Times*
> > August 26, 1905 – President Takes Plunge in Submarine

Chapter 8 - Variations on a Theme

Newspaper Archives - Proquest Archives. *The New York Times* – www.nytimes.com

> *Gazette & Bulletin*
> > August 26, 1905 – The President Takes Plunge in Submarine

The Arizona Republican
     August 26, 1905 – President Submerged

The Christian Herald
     September 15, 1905 – The President's Submarine Trip

The Constitution
     August 26, 1905 – Roosevelt Dives Beneath Billows

The Daily Courier
     August 26, 1905 – Chief Takes a Dive

The Daily Northwestern
     August 26, 1905 – Tests of the Plunger

The Fort Wayne Journal Gazette
     August 26, 1905 – In Submarine Boat President Roosevelt
     Plunged into Long Island Sound

The Fort Wayne Sentinel
     August 26, 1905 – President Goes to Bottom of Ocean

The Marion Daily Star
     August 26, 1905 – Roosevelt Under Sea

The Massillon Independent
     August 26, 1905 –Chief Takes a Dive

The New York Times
     August 26, 1905 – President Takes Plunge in Submarine

The Oakland Tribune
     August 10, 1905 – President May Dive

The Post Standard
     August 26, 1905 – Roosevelt under Waves of Ocean for Fifty
     Minutes

The Washington Post
     August 26, 1905 - At Bottom of Sound

<u>Chapter 9 - Shots across the bow</u>

Newspaper Archives - Proquest Archives. *The New York Times* – www.nytimes.com

    The Agitator
        August 29, 1905 – Editorial

    The Colorado Springs Gazette
        August 29, 1905 – The President and the Plunger

    The Constitution
        August 27, 1905 – Editorial – The Submarine's Greatest Triumph
        August 27, 1905 – tidbit of information

    The Fort Wayne Weekly Sentinel
        August 30, 1905 – Knabenshue to Ask President to Fly

    The New York Times
        August 27, 1905 – Our Submerged President

Chapter 10 - Advocate for a Naval Hero

Morison, Samuel Eliot. *John Paul Jones – A Sailor's Biography*. Time Incorporated. Time Reading Program Special Edition. New York, N.Y. 1959.

Newspaper Archives - *The New York Times* – www.nytimes.com

    The New York Times
        November 20, 1903 – To Honor John Paul Jones
        February 14, 1905 – Plea For Heroes
        February 25, 1905 – Bones of John Paul Jones
        February 25, 1905 – Special to the New York Times – Washington Report
        February 27, 1905 – Not Paul Jones's Coffin
        April 15, 1905 – Washington – April 14th
        April 18, 1905 – In Honor of Paul Jones
        April 22, 1905 – To Bring Back Hero's Body
        April 23, 1905 – At Odds Over Paul Jones
        May 2, 1905 – To Preserve Jones's Body
        July 25, 1905 – Jones' Body Entombed at the Naval Academy
        January 21, 1906 – Huge Petition Delivered
        April 25, 1906 – Two Nations at Bier of John Paul Jones

Sweetman, Jack. *American Naval History – An Illustrated Chronology of the U.S. Navy and Marine Corps, 1775 – Present*. Naval Institute Press. Annapolis, Maryland. 1991 – second edition. First published in 1984.

The Book of the Navy. Doubleday, Doran & Company, Inc. U.S.A. 1944.

Chapter 11 - Foundations of a Naval Legacy

Newspaper Archives - *The New York Times* – www.nytimes.com

The New York Times
August 18, 1903 – Destroyers Crash at Naval Review
January 15, 1904 – President on Naval Militia
October 13, 1904 – Roosevelt's Sea Power Talk
February 23, 1905 – Washington Favored Great Navy - Roosevelt
May 11, 1905 – Urges Navy for Peace
August 27, 1905 – Crews of Submarines to Receive More Pay
November 1, 1905 – Roosevelt Shoveled Coal on Big Cruiser
August 25, 1906 – Editorial – The Naval Review
September 4, 1906 – Fleets Array a Grand Sight
September 30, 1906 - Roosevelt Sits Down with Sailors at Mess
August 16, 1908 – Seaman Insulted Roosevelt
Sept. 23, 1908 – Saucy Card to Roosevelt

Chapter 12 - The Atlantic Fleet

Gable, John Allen. *America's 26th President – Theodore Roosevelt – Famous American Series*. Eastern National Publishing Company. 2003.

Love, Robert William Jr. *TR's Big Stick: Roosevelt and the Navy, 1901-1909*. Naylor, Natalie A., Brinkley, Douglas, Gable, John Allen, Editors. *Theodore Roosevelt – Many-sided American*. Long Island Studies Institute. Hofstra University. Hempstead, New York. 1992.

McKinley, Mike. *The Cruise of the Great White Fleet*. Article. Navy Department Library. Department of the Navy. United States Naval Historical Society. Available online.

Newspaper Archives - *The New York Times* – www.nytimes.com

The New York Times
April 27, 1907 – President Stops Panic at Fair
June 10, 1907 – Roosevelt at Jamestown

July 23, 1908 – President Demands Hard-Hitting Navy
November 13, 1908 – No Marines On Ships
March 4, 1909 – Roosevelt's Last Acts

Reckner, James R. *The Rebirth of the Fleet.* Article. *Naval History Magazine.* December 2007. United States Naval Institute. Annapolis, Maryland.

United States Naval Historical Society. U.S. Navy Department. *Information Relative to the Voyage of the United States Atlantic Fleet Around the World, December 16, 1907 to February 22, 1909.* Government Printing Office. Washington, D.C. 1910. Available online.

Chapter 13 - East Meets West

Dolan, Edward F., *Panama and the United States, Their Canal, Their Stormy Years.* Franklin Watts Publishing Company, New York., 1990.

Morris, Edmund. *The Rise of Theodore Roosevelt.* Random House, Inc. New York, N.Y. Modern Library Paperback Edition. 2001. First edition published by Coward, McCann & Geoghegan, 1979.

Newspaper Archives - *The New York Times* – www.nytimes.com

The New York Times
June 23, 1905 – Big Navy or No Canal Roosevelt Declares

Chapter 14 - The Lasting Legacy

Newspaper Archives - *The New York Times* – www.nytimes.com

The New York Times
May 23, 1906 – Kaiser May be Submerged
November 22, 1914 – The Navy as a Peacemaker
October 28, 1922 – Navy and Roosevelt Honored in Capital

The Theodore Roosevelt Association Website. *TR and the Navy. Edward J. Renehan speech from October 29, 1999.* Available online.

United States Naval Historical Center. U.S. Navy Department. *Dictionary of American Naval Fighting Ships.* Available online.

United States Naval Historical Center. U.S. Navy Department. *U.S. Navy Active Ship Force Levels 1886-2000.* Available online.

Conclusion

Auchincloss, Louis. *Theodore Roosevelt*. The American Presidents Series. Arthur M. Schlesinger, Jr., General Editor. Times Books. Henry Holt and Company. New York, New York. 2001.

Collier, Peter. *The Roosevelts – An American Saga*. Simon & Schuster. New York, N.Y. 1994.

Gilbert, Martin. *D-Day*. John Wiley & Sons, Inc. Hoboken, N.J. 2004.

Newspaper Archives - *The New York Times* – www.nytimes.com

> *The New York Times*
> October 27, 1923 – Navy Day and Roosevelt Day

United States Naval Historical Center. U.S. Navy Department. *Dictionary of American Naval Fighting Ships*. Available online.

Epilogue

Morris, Edmund. *Theodore Rex*. Random House, Inc. New York, N.Y. 2001

Newspaper Archives - *The New York Times* – www.nytimes.com

> *The New York Times*
> January 24, 1906 – Our Navy Best - Roosevelt

The Theodore Roosevelt Association Website. *Treaty of Portsmouth & The Nobel Prize*. Available online.

Appendices

Appendix A   Further Information

A. *U.S.S. Plunger*

> United States Naval Historical Center. U.S. Navy Department. *Dictionary of American Naval Fighting Ships*. Available online.

> Newspaper Archives - *The New York Times* – www.nytimes.com

> > *The New York Times*
> > May 20, 1903 – Submarine Boat Tests

April 14, 1908 – Plunger's Record Run
August 17, 1913 – Plunger Will Be Warships'
Target
December 17, 1921 – Former Prides of Navy
Inspected as Junk

T.A. Scott Collection. (Coll. 1, Box 21/16) *Documents relating to the submarine PLUNGER.* G.W. Blunt White Library. Mystic Seaport Museum. Mystic, C.T.

B. Lt. Nelson

Newspaper Archives - *The New York Times* – www.nytimes.com

The New York Times
April 17, 1904 – Lieut. Nelson's Punishment
November 20, 1905 – Took President Diving,
Restored to Rank
March 4, 1907 – Middies to Study the
Submarine
March 17, 1907 – Submarine Boats off for
Annapolis
August 10, 1910 – Junk Pile the Fate of Historic
Warship

United States Naval Historical Center. U.S. Navy Department. *Dictionary of American Naval Fighting Ships.* Available online.

Appendix B - Vessel Specifics

United States Naval Historical Center. U.S. Navy Department. *Dictionary of American Naval Fighting Ships.* Available online.

Appendix C - U.S. Navy Active Ship Levels 1898-1916

Newspaper Archives - *The New York Times* – www.nytimes.com

Fort Wayne Journal-Gazette
September 4, 1915 - The Cost of the Army and Navy

The New York Times
May 27, 1906 – Naval Budget Increased

United States Naval Historical Center. U.S. Navy Department. *U.S. Navy Active Ship Force Levels 1886-2000.* Available online.

Appendix D - John Paul Jones – Hero Unwanted?

Armbruster, Eugene L., *The Wallabout Prison Ships, 1776-1783*, Private Printing by the Author, Limited to 300 copies, New York, 1920. Pages 5-7.

Grafton, John. *The American Revolution – A Picture Sourcebook*, Dover Publications Inc., New York, 1975. Pages 278-282.

Morison, Samuel Eliot., *John Paul Jones, A Sailor's Biography*, Time Incorporated, New York, 1959.

Roberts, W. Adolphe and Brentano, Lowell., *The Book of the Navy*, Doubleday & Company, Garden City, New York, 1944. Pages 4-18.

Waldo, S. Putnam., *Biographical Sketches of Distinguished American Naval Heroes in the War of the Revolution, Between the American Republic and the Kingdom of Great Britain*, Kennikat Press, Port Washington, New York, Originally published in1823 (reprinted in 1970). Pages 75-84.

Appendix A – Additional Information

The following information is provided for the benefit of the reader. Sources are listed in the references section.

U.S.S. Plunger (A-1)

The keel of the *Plunger* submarine was laid down on May 21, 1901 at the Crescent Shipyard in Elizabethport, N.J. The submarine was being built at the facility under sub-contractual agreement by the John P. Holland Torpedo Boat Company of New York. On February 1, 1902, the completed torpedo boat was launched. On May 19, 1903 the *Plunger* and her sister submarine *Shark* completed some of their "official Government trails on Peconic Bay." (*NYT*, 20MAY1903) The trials included an underwater run over a two mile long course that ended with a torpedo shot at a target. "The *Plunger* exceeded the Government requirements in speed and fired the torpedo with absolute accuracy between two flag buoys representing the vitals of a battleship."[68] (*NYT*, 20MAY1903) After tests and trials were completed, the *Plunger* was commissioned at the Holland Company facility located in New Suffolk, Long Island on September 19, 1903. At the helm and acting as the boat's first skipper was Lieutenant Charles P. Nelson.

The *Plunger* was originally "assigned to the Naval Torpedo Station" located in Newport, Rhode Island, for her first tow years, primarily acting as a training platform for other submarine boat crew that were being added to the fleet. She also was engaged in "experimental torpedo week" with the exception of a nine month overhaul "between March and November of 1904." (DANFS) During this part of her career she operated under normal conditions. But the fate of the little *Plunger* submarine was about to change when her skipper received orders to prepare her for a review by President Roosevelt. A review of the boat's

---

[68] The *Shark* did not meet the necessary requirements of speed due to a "hot bearing," but the torpedo shot was right on target. (*NYT*, 20MAY1903)

log books during the week and a half prior to the historic trip were complete with leaks, late night repairs, fresh paint and a lot of hard work. On the 25th of August, the *Plunger* and her crew performed admirably and within a few short hours, helped solidify presidential support for the fledgling submarine service.

Following the successful trails for the Commander-In-Chief, the *Plunger* returned to her normal duties until she was decommissioned on November 3, 1905. She "remained inactive until recommissioned on 23 February 1907, Lt. Guy W.S. Castle in command." (DANFS) Less than one month later, the *Plunger* joined her sister submarines *Porpoise* and *Shark* as part of the "first submarine flotilla, based at the New York Navy Yard." (DANFS) In March of 1907, the flotilla was transferred to teach midshipmen at the Naval Academy, submarine technology. By the following April, it appears that the time in southern waters was completed. On April 13, 1908, the *Plunger* made a historic "record run" from the New York Navy Yard to the Newport, Rhode Island torpedo boat station averaging "8 knots an hour" in "a rough sea" with a blowing gale. (*NYT*, 14APR1908) The total trip was made in 17 ½ hours with Lieutenant Bassett in command of the submarine at the time. In early May 1909, the *Plunger* received a new skipper, Ensign Chester W. Nimitz.[69] The following fall in October 1909, the *Plunger* was "reassigned to the Charleston (S.C.) Navy Yard." Less than six months later, she was placed in the reserve torpedo division, and was "renamed *A-1* (Submarine Torpedo Boat No. 2) on 17 November 1911." (DANFS) According to an August 17, 1913 article, the *Plunger* was to be towed, unceremoniously from her mooring in South Carolina, to the waters north of the Mason-Dixon Line to be "offered as a sacrifice to test the marksmanship of the gunners of the Atlantic Fleet." (*NYT*, 17AUG1913)

---

[69] Nimitz later commented on the early submarine boats in which he served. The submarines he said were "a cross between a Jules Verne fantasy and a humpbacked whale." (DANFS)

The thought of using one of the first submarines of the United States Navy as a target, after a distinguished and historic career raised cane with many officers within the naval ranks. "She will make a good target," the author of the article stated, "but there are hundreds of naval men who think she would make a much better relic." (*NYT*, 17AUG1913) The calls to keep the submarine in reserve or to preserve her for posterity fell upon deaf ears. The *Plunger*, "having been authorized for use as an 'experimental target'…[was] designated as 'Target E' on 29 August 1916. Ultimately hoisted on board the hulk of the former monitor *Puritan*, the partially dismantled torpedo boat was authorized for sale on 25 August 1921, on an 'where is, as is' basis. She was sold for scrap on 26 January 1922."[70] (DANFS)

The records of the United States Navy end with her sale, but the fate of the *Plunger* did not end on that late day in January of 1922. A subsequent search of commercial and military records indicate that the *Plunger*, between her use as a target in 1916 and before being "sold" by the United States Navy, was sold and then purchased again by the government for use as a training tool for divers. The documents, part of the T.A. Scott Collection, archived in the G.W. Blount White Library of the Mystic Seaport Museum, provide insight into the time period through a series of correspondence between the United States Navy and the T.A. Scott Company.[71] The first letter, dated March 22, 1918, includes typed stenographer noted pages of a conversation between Mr. Scott and one of his

---

[70] The sale of the *Plunger* took place during a large sell-off of obsolete naval craft and vessels which included the battleships *Maine*, *Missouri*, *Wisconsin*, and several monitors. The "cheapest of the lot" was the "monitor *Puritan* which aboard her was the *A-1 Plunger*." The appraised value was $4,000. (*NYT*, 21DEC1921) The *Wisconsin*, "which was built in San Francisco in 1908" at a cost between three and five million dollars was "appraised as junk at $120,000." (*NYT*, 17DEC1921)

[71] The T.A. Scott Company was one of the three largest salvage companies in the northeast during the era. The Scott Company would eventually merge with the Merritt-Chapman Salvage Company to form the Merritt-Chapman & Scott Company in 1922. A brief history of the Merritt-Chapman & Scott Company is available in *Claimed by the Sea – Long Island Shipwrecks, Appendix A*.

associates, Mr. Smith. The crux of the conversation is the attempt by Mr. Scott to be awarded a contract to remove the submarine from its watery grave.

A *Proposal For Supplies or Services* form completed by a United States Navy Paymaster from the United States Navy Yard in Brooklyn, N.Y., addressed to the T.A. Scott Company in New London, Connecticut, indicated that a bid must be made for the salvage of "1 Steel or Iron Hulk, approximately 100 feet long for $2200.00." A subsequent form, Part of requisition Number 422-Bu explains that a request was made by the Bureau Construction & Repair for the hulks use in connection with an extension of salvage facilities. The form also reminds the bidder that the cylindrical hull was "approximately 85' long by 16' at its widest diameter."

A telephone report recorded the conversation between Captain Cable and Mr. Smith on March 23, 1918. Mr. Smith asks how much Captain Cable is willing to sell the *Plunger* to him for. Captain Cable responds that it is for sale for $500.00. An interesting exchange begins:

Smith: She is sunk, isn't she?

Cable: Yes. I think the top of her hull is out of the water, only shoal water.

Smith: Are there any holes in the hull that you know of?

Cable: Must be or she wouldn't have sunk.

The response from the officer requires a good laugh. The conversation indicates that the submarine was just a shell as her insides and machinery had been removed. Smith requests a week to think about the purchase to which Cable agrees.

A handwritten note from a Mr. A.F. Mix, on Hotel Manhattan stationary, on March 24, 1918, follows the salvage efforts of the hulk. Mr. Mix reports to his superiors that he completed a survey of the submarine. He is unable to determine the cause of the sinking, but indicates that some of the sea cocks were opened but that other areas were rusted and open as well. He also reported that no superstructure was present, but that due to mud inside the hulk, he could not determine whether or not any of the machinery of her engines was still present. His final observation was that "unless we strike a very low tide, the boat will have to be lifted."

On March 26th, 1918, Mr. Smith again telephones Captain Cable and tells him that he sold the submarine to Mr. Scott, whom he refers to as Captain Scott. At this point the deal was closed. Mr. Smith again asks if anything is in the submarine, but Captain Cable again replies that she is empty and that it is just the shell. Captain Cable asks Mr. Smith to contact him so that he could "go over there with you." Mr. Smith then refers to the submarine once again at the closing of the conversation by asking Captain Cable the following question, "That is the one you showed us the picture of in your office the other day?" Captain Cable replies, "No, that is the old "Holland." Smith ends the phone conversation with "All right."

After his conversation with Captain Cable was concluded, Mr. Smith contacted his associate Mr. Mix. The two men decide on how they are going to raise the submarine and discuss other matters of business. Mr. Mix also indicated that during his inspection of the boat, he felt something in the hulk that he thought might be the batteries.

A document dated April 4, 1918 provides additional insight into the fate of the submarine. Confirming that the work would continue, it indicates the confirmed requisition for the submarine. The deal had been sealed and sent. Smith and Mix had their work cut out for them. On April 6, 1918, Mr. Mix received a telegram at the Edgewater Hotel in Halesite, Long Island, from the T.A. Scott Company informing him to send a diver and tender to Boston immediately and for him to report to New London for a physical examination. The next telegram was sent April 9, and was from Capt. Nixon stating that the submarine was floated and that he was requesting two boats, Addie and Carrie to be sent to the site so that they can tow the boat to New London.

On official T.A. Scott Company Incorporated Stationary, the bill of sale to the United States Navy is recorded on April 15, 1918. The T.A. Scott Company had successfully raised, towed, and delivered the *Plunger* to its new owner, the United States Navy.

A few weeks passed and Mr. Smith received a phone call from a Submarine Supply officer from New London. The supply officer was confused as to what the old submarine was being supplied for. The conversation is an excellent example of the left hand not knowing what the right hand is doing.

Supply O: What was that supplied for?

Smith: For the Salvage Diving School, that is down here, using it just north of our dock.

Supply O: Who used it?

Smith: Salvage Diving School.

Supply O: I see.

Smith: That is really the hull of the old submarine *Plunger*?

Supply O: Who placed the order for that hull?

Smith: The Pay Office at the Brooklyn Navy Yard.

Supply O: That is under the Naval District Base?

Smith: I am sure I don't know. We sent the bill to them because they sent us the order.

Supply O: That is right.

Smith: If you would like to have a copy of the original order we will be glad to send it to you.

Supply O: Want to get a drift of the thing, don't know anything about it, nobody here seems to know. Everything for New London arrives on my desk. I know something unofficially about this Diving School, but somebody else handles it. Wanted to send it along so you can get your money.

Smith: Thank you, we will appreciate it very much.

The last piece of paperwork in the file contained a letter from the T.A. Scott Company to the District Salvage Officer, United States Navy, at New London, Connecticut. Sent on December 6th, 1918, the letter, from the manager of the T.A. Scott Company stated, "Would respectfully call your attention to the Submarine "Plunger" now sunk in the vicinity of White Rock. Said submarine constitutes a menace to navigation, being entirely submerged and not marked. As you are aware, the vessel is sunk in fairway leading to our storage place on White Rock." The letter concludes in a positive way, as the manager offers his company's assistance in rectifying the situation.

So as of December 6, 1918, the original *Plunger* submarine, or what was left of her was in the waters off of White Rock in Connecticut. Unfortunately the trail of paperwork on the *Plunger* submarine ends – with the exception of the final date of sale by the U.S. Government in 1922. Though several discrepancies exist between the dimensions provided throughout the course of correspondences between the T.A. Scott Company, the United States Navy, most specifically regarding the length and beam of the submerged hulk, it is quite possible, considering the known timeline that the *Plunger* submarine, after a distinguished career in the United States Navy, (after being a target, after having sunk, and after being sold and salvaged by a commercial salvage company) once again became the property of the United States Navy, for a short period of time before finally being sold as scrap in 1922. The fate of the *Plunger* or what remained of her after that time frame, remains clouded in mystery.

Deck Logs of the *U.S.S.T.B. Plunger* – August 13th, 1905-September 1, 1905

The following information was transcribed from photocopies of the original log book of the *U.S.S.T.B.* (Torpedo Boat) *Plunger*. The original logs were handwritten therefore; any and all inaccuracies during the transcribing process are the responsibility of the author. Special thanks to Kim McKeithan, National Archives and Records Administration for her assistance in locating the original log book pages.

Sunday, August 13th

Weather rain, Wind N.N.E. Barometer 3.24. Men from C+R Dept. working in boat, 3 plumbers + 2 helpers, and worked all night. Air line still leaking. All air and water gauges belong to the boat were repaired and installed.

Monday, August 14th

Weather fair, Wind N.N.E. barometer, 30.26. Men from C+R Dept. working in boat. 3 plumbers + 2 helpers, 3 machinists + 1 helper. Men worked all night air line still leaking.

Tuesday, August 15th

Weather fair, Wind N. Barometer 30.28. Men from C+R Dept. Working in boat, 3 plumbers + 2 helpers, 2 machinists + 1 helper, worked all night. Took off manhole plate on forward Kingston jacket, found gasoline tank bulkhead leading, gasoline had high pressure. Air line could not be made to stand 2000 lbs., but stood 1500 lbs. with the few small leaks, which were patched up with *illegible* so as to hold 1500 lbs. without any leaks.

Wednesday, August 16th

Weather fair, Wind N.N.W. Barometer 36.27. Men from C+R Dept. working in boat, 1 plumber + 1 helper, 2 machinists + 1 helper, 2 corkers worked all night. Pumped 16 lbs. of gasoline out of gasoline tank. Took manhole plates off of gasoline tank, washed, and aired tank thoroughly with blowers. Corkers working on gasoline tank.

Thursday, August 17th

Weather fair, Wind N.N.W. Barometer 30.27. Men from C+R Dept. worked in boat, 1 plumber + 1 helper, 2 machinists + 1 helper, 2 corkers, worked all night. 2 electrical machinists working on rheostat. Corkers working on gasoline tanks. Put up periscope.

Friday, August 18th

Weather fair, wind N.E. Barometer, 30.26. Men from C+R Dept. working in boat, 1 plumber + 1 helper, 2 machinists + 1 helper, 2 corkers Put manhole plates on tanks and tested tanks with 10 lbs. air pressure, formed a few small leaks around, with leaks which were patched up with litharge. Put gasoline in tank. Electricians belong to the boat, pumped acid out of six cells in forward batteries and refilled same with new acid.

Saturday, August 19th

Weather cloudy, Wind x. Barometer 30.19. Men from C+R Dept. working in boat, 2 machinists + 1 helper, 2 electrical machinists working on spark breakers from Equip. Dept. Stowed lead ballast in forward Kingston well. Put new rubber gaskets on all ventilator flaps. Machinists with compressor gearing.

Sunday, August 20th

Weather fair, Wind N. by E. Barometer 30.27. men from Equip. Dept. 2 electricians. Machinists worked on gas engine for 15 minutes.

Monday, August 21st

Weather fair, Wind N.E. Barometer 30.24. Men from Equip. Dept. working on field coils, took out 2 upper field coils and rewound them. Two (2) machinists mates from S.E. Dept. working on gasoline engine circulating *illegible*. Electricians worked all night. Put in 6 lbs. of gasoline. Put all stores aboard the Tug Apache. Received our requisition from General Store-Keeper. 100 gals. of engine oil, 100 lbs. of cotton waste, 30 lbs. saltwater soap, 12 cans of lacquer luster + 12 sheets of No. 2 Emery cloth.

Tuesday, August 22nd

Weather fair. Wind N.E. Barometer 30.24. Ran boat with nose alongside of dock for 30 minutes. Left doc under tow of Apache at 2.10 P.M. for Oyster Bay, arrived at 6.20 P.M. Moored alongside of tug. Charged batteries for 2 hours.

Wednesday, August 23rd

Weather fair, Wind N.N. W. Barometer 30.26. Charged four (4) flasks of air to 1200 lbs. Trimmed boat, left tug, went out in Bay under motor, trimmed down and made three (3) short dies. Returned to tug and secured alongside. Charged batteries.

Thursday, August 24th

Weather fair, Wind N. Barometer 30.21. Charged batteries and charged air to 1000 lbs. in all flasks. Put torpedo in boat and charged same with air to 1230 lbs. Cleaned all stations, painted outside of boat. Compressor shaft carried away. Gasket on No. 3 cylinder of gas engine leaking bad.

Friday, August 25th

Weather rain, Wind E.S.E. Barometer 30.08. Charged batteries for 2 hours. Left tug, trimmed down in bay and made five short dives, pumped out tanks, returned and secured alongside of tug. Charged batteries for 3 ½ hours. At 3.30 P.M. President Roosevelt came on board, left tug and ran out to Sound under gas-engine, trimmed down at 4.10 P.M. and made a series of dives, pumped all tanks. At 5.15 returned to bay under gas engine and secured alongside of tug. Put torpedo in tug, charged batteries. President left boat at 6.10 P.M.

Saturday, August 26th

Weather cloudy, Wind S.E. Barometer 30.18. Charged batteries for 2 hours. Left tug and trimmed down in Bay, made short dive and fired a torpedo, pumped tanks, ran out to Sound under gas-engine, trimmed down, made a series of dives, pumped tanks, returned to Bay under gas-engine and secured alongside of tug. Charged batteries.

Sunday, August 27th

Weather rain, Wind S. Barometer 30.20. Ventilated boat + batteries.

Monday, August 28th

Weather fair. Wind N.W. Barometer 30.24 Left Oyster Bay under tow of Apache at 8.20 A.M. Running under three (3) cylinders on gas-engine for 35 minutes. Had to shut down gas-engine on account of gear on governor shaft carrying away. Arrived in N.Y. at 11. 55 A.M. Secured to docks.

Tuesday, August 29th

Weather fair, Wind N.W. Barometer 30.27. Took all stores off tug and put in Building #137. Crew returned to *Hancock* with bags + hammocks.

Wednesday, August 30th

Weather fair, Wind S.W. Barometer 30.24. Cleaned all stations and boat. Charged batteries from Yard Plant.

Thursday, August 31st

Weather fair, Wind S.S. W. Barometer 30.24. Cleaned stations and boat. Discharged batteries on propeller with boat secured to dock. 1 plumber + 1 helper + 2 machinist from C+R Dept. working in boat. Charged batteries during night from Yard Plant.

Friday, September 1st

Weather fair, Wind N.E. Barometer 30.25. Cleaned all stations. Discharged batteries on propeller with boat secured to dock. Added water to all cells in forward batteries. 1 plumber, 1 helper, + 2 machinists from C+R Dept. working in boat. Charged batteries during night from Yard Plant.

Lieutenant Charles Preston Nelson

Born in Baltimore, Maryland on February 5, 1877, Charles Preston Nelson was appointed a naval cadet on May 19, 1894. His appointment marked the beginning of a thirty-nine year career in the United States Navy. After his training was completed, he graduated in time for the hostilities of the Spanish-American War in 1898 where he participated "in the blockade and battle of Santiago, Cuba." (DANFS) From Cuba, Nelson was transferred to the Philippines where he served "during the insurrection." (DANFS) From the Far East, Nelson took a position "with the torpedo boat training command." (DANFS) Though all seemed to be going well for the young officer, one incident threatened to mare his ability to make the United States Navy a career. On April 16, 1904, Lieutenant Junior Grade (LTJG) Nelson stood before the military court martial and learned that he was found responsible for "culpable negligence and inefficiency in the performance of duties in connection with the collision of the torpedo boat *Winslow* and the ferry boat *America* in the East River, at New York," in December 1903.[72] (*NYT*, 17APR1904) His sentence was the loss of three numbers for promotion and reprimand. The punishment however marked the young officer's career and eventually he was placed in charge of a submarine – an aspect of the fleet that in her fledging years was not highly-respected by naval officers.

While commanding the *U.S.S. Plunger*, however, Lt. Nelson would find the case reviewed by none other than his Commander-in-Chief, Roosevelt. A few days after the historic trip, Roosevelt returned to Washington and began a review of the incident. "He investigated the affair and was convinced that the young

---

[72] The *Winslow* had the unfortunate distinction of being the stage for the first American serviceman killed in the Spanish-American War. Ensign Bagley, in command of the *Winslow* was killed while "directing the handling of his boat from the deck. He was besides the little starboard gun encouraging his men when a shell exploded at his feet." The *Winslow* was slated for sale as scrap in August of 1910. (*NYT*, 10AUG1910)

officer should be exonerated." (*NYT*, 20NOV1905) Soon after, Lieutenant Nelson was exonerated and restored to his original place on the promotion list.

In addition to commanding the *U.S.S. Plunger*, Nelson also served as the commanding officer of the *U.S.S. Porpoise*, one of the *U.S.S. Plunger*'s sister boats. In 1907 Nelson took a small flotilla, including the *U.S.S. Plunger*, "sometimes referred to as the 'President's Own,' the *Porpoise* and the *Shark*," to Annapolis, Maryland.[73] (*NYT*, 4MAR1907) The submarines were utilized to teach midshipmen the newest additions to the fleet. "Since the President's memorable trip to the bottom of the Long Island Sound his interest in the submarine has not diminished and the new departure the outcome of which will be that practically every midshipman at Annapolis will get a liberal schooling under water to be due to his personal influence and interest in the terrible little engines of war." (*NYT*, 4MAR1907) After several years in the submarine service, Nelson was "First Lieutenant of [the] *Illinois* and later of [the] *Ohio*." (DANFS) During the First World War, while in command of the *Leonidas*, "a tender for submarine chasers," Nelson was also charged with commanding "submarine chaser divisions ordered to Corfu, Greece." During this time period, "twelve of the submarine chasers under his command participated with the British and Italian naval forces in the destruction of the Austrian naval base at Durazzo on 3 October 1918, during which two submarines were destroyed." (DANFS) As a result of his actions during this risky and dangerous operation, Nelson was "awarded the Distinguished Service Medal and several foreign decorations." (DANFS) Following the end of hostilities, Nelson served in the "3rd and 4th Naval Districts" from 1919 to 1929. "In January 1929 he was appointed coordinator of the Seattle area, in which capacity he served until he retired as Rear Admiral" on June 30, 1933. (DANFS) Rear Admiral Nelson died on November 16, 1935.

---

[73] On March 17, 1907, the submarines *Plunger*, *Porpoise* and *Shark*, accompanied by the "naval tugs *Nina* and *Pontiac*" cruised to the waters to be utilized at the Naval Academy. (*NYT*, 17MAR1907)

***U.S.S. Nelson.* Courtesy – U.S. Navy.**

The United States Navy's *DD-623's* keel was laid on May 7, 1942 and named in honor of Nelson's contributions as a naval officer. The vessel was sponsored by "Mrs. Nelson Stewart, daughter of Rear Admiral Charles Preston Nelson." (DANFS) The *Nelson* would serve throughout World War II and in January 1947, she was placed out of commission and placed in reserve as part of the U.S. Atlantic Reserve Fleet. The *Nelson* was finally struck from the naval register on March 1, 1968 and sold in July 1969. (DANFS)

Appendix B – Vessel Specifics

The following information provides specific details and characteristics to some of the vessels and craft discussed in the preceding chapters. Sources are listed in the references section. All photographs courtesy of the United States Naval Historical Center Archives.

U.S.S. Plunger

Type of Vessel	Adder Class Submarine
Length	63 feet, 10 inches
Beam	11 feet, 11 inches
Draft	10 feet, 7 inches
Displacement	Surface – 107 tons
	Submerged – 123 tons
Year Built	Keel Laid on 21MAY01
Where Built	Crescent Shipyards, Elizabethport, N.J.
Engine Type	Otto Gasoline Engine Works (160 HP)
Propulsion Type	1 single screw, Electro-Dynamic Electric Motors
	(150 HP)
Fuel Capacity	767 gallons
Battery Cells	60
Speed	Surface – 8 knots
	Submerged – 7 knots
Depth Limit	150 feet
Armament	1 torpedo tube
Crew Complement	1 officer, 6 enlisted crew
Hailing Port(s)	various
Launched	1FEB02
Commissioned	19SEP03 at Holland Co. New Suffolk, Long Island, NY.
De-Commissioned	3NOV05
Re-Commissioned	7MAR07
Renamed	U.S.S. A-1 (Submarine Torpedo Boat #2) on 17NOV11
Final Disposition	Struck from Naval Register on 24FEB16
	Designated as experimental "target E" on 29AUG16
	Sold for scrapping on 26JAN22

U.S.S. Apache

Type of Vessel	Naval Tug
Length	141 feet, 6 inches
Beam	29 feet
Draft	10 feet
Year Built	1889
Where Built	Tottenville, New York
Builder	A.C. Brown
Speed	10 knots
Armament	2, 1 pounder, 1 machine gun which were added in 1918
Hailing Port(s)	Norfolk, VA Navy Yard, Key West, FL, New York Navy Yard and Iona Island, NY and Charleston, SC
Commissioned	June 11, 1898
Acquired	Purchased by the Navy from Merritt & Chapman Wrecking Co. on May 24, 1898.
Re-Named	*Aspinet* on April 11, 1918
Re-Designated	YF-176 on July 17, 1920*
Decommissioned	September 24, 1898, but refitted for service in 1900.
Final Disposition	Sold in Charleston, SC on September 29, 1925

The *U.S.S. Apache* was originally named the *J.D. Jones*. It was renamed *Apache* and commissioned in 1898. Assigned originally to the Norfolk Navy Yard, the Apache spent time in Key West, Florida during the Spanish-American War and then returned to Norfolk, V.A. where she was decommissioned. In 1900, the *U.S.S. Apache* was refitted for service at Iona Island in New York and was assigned to the New York Navy Yard and Iona Island until 1920. Now known as the *Aspinet*, she was assigned to Charleston, South Carolina and listed as a District Craft. She became *YF-176* in that same year and was sold in Charleston on September 25, 1929.

*In 1920, the United States Navy went to an alphanumeric hull numbering system.

151

Presidential Yacht *Sylph*

Type of Vessel	Converted yacht used as a Presidential yacht.
Length	123 feet, 8 inches
Beam	20 feet
Year Built	1898
Where Built	Chester, Pennsylvania
Builder	John Roach & Company
Engine Type	steam engines. Later replaced with a 400 HP Worthington Diesel engine – 1935.
Speed	15 knots with original steam engines
Hailing Port(s)	Norfolk, VA and Washington, DC Navy Yards
Commissioned	August 18, 1898 at the Norfolk Navy Yard
Re-Designated	*PY-5* on July 17, 1921
De-Commissioned	April 29, 1929
Final Disposition	Sold to Frank G. Blair of Brooklyn, NY on November 26, 1929. Later was used as fishing boat and a ferry. The hulk was sold when the owners defaulted on their mortgage – final fate unknown.

The *Slyph*, the third naval vessel to carry the name, was utilized as a yacht for the President and other high officials. It was first used by President McKinley and was last used by President Woodrow Wilson. President Roosevelt also utilized the *U.S.S. Mayflower* as a presidential yacht.

Presidential Yacht – *U.S.S. Mayflower*

Type of Vessel	Converted yacht used as a Presidential yacht
Length	273 feet
Beam	36 feet
Draft	13 feet, 2 inches
Displacement	2,690 tons
Year Built	1896
Where Built	Clydebank, Scotland
Builder	J. and O. Thompson
Engine Type	2 400 HP triple expansion, 4 cylinder, double acting steam engines with two shafts.
Speed	17 knots
Armament	6, 6 pounders, one 5 inch 51, two 3 inch 50, six 20 mm, two DCT, four Y guns, 1 hedge hog.
Hailing Port(s)	Various
Acquired	Purchased by the U.S. Navy in 1898
Commissioned	*U.S.S. Mayflower* on March 24, 1898
De-Commissioned	November 1, 1904
Re-Commissioned	July 25, 1905 as a presidential yacht
Re-Designated	*PY-1* on July 17, 1920
De-Commissioned	March 22, 1929
Fate	Sold to various owners between World War I and World War II. Purchased by the War Shipping Administration on July 31, 1942 and renamed Butte.
Transferred	From the WSA to the United States Coast Guard on September 6, 1943.
Re-Commissioned	USCGC Mayflower, WPG-183 on October 19, 1943
De-Commissioned	July 1, 1946 and returned to the WSA.
Final Disposition	Unknown

The *U.S.S. Mayflower* was originally named the *Ogden Goelet* and had been built for use as a yacht in European waters. Purchased by the United States Navy in 1898, the *Mayflower* had a rich history in service as both a Presidential Yacht as well as a United States Coast Guard Cutter. After it was finally decommissioned for the last time after World War II, the *Mayflower* was sold to various owners and she was utilized for as an artic seal catcher, a coastal trader, and provided refuge for Jewish refugees from the ill-fated *Exodus* to Haifa, Palestine. Her final fate is unknown.

Appendix C - U.S. Navy Active Ship Levels 1898-1916

Roosevelt had been preaching the necessity of a strong naval power since his publication in 1883 of *The Naval War of 1812* and during his position as the Assistant Secretary of the Navy in 1897-1898. Once President in 1901 the United States Navy was ranked fifth in the World, but by the time he left office in 1909, the United States Navy was second only to the British Royal Navy. The expansion of the Navy had increased due to multiple factors including the Spanish-American war and Roosevelt leadership, as indicated in the following United States Navy Active Ship Level statistics from the U.S. Naval Historical Center.

December 1898

Battleships	6
Cruisers	18
Monitor	14
Destroyers	0
Torpedo Boats	12
Steam gunboats	34
Auxiliaries	30
Screw Steamers	16
Screw Sloops	4
Sailing Ships	1
Gunboats	25
Steel Navy*	114
Old Navy**	46
Total Active	160

*Steel Navy – Steel hulled triple expansion steam engine warships. (standard ships of 20th century navies.)
**Old Navy – Iron-hulled vessels utilizing early steam engines.

December 1903

Battleships	11
Cruisers	19
Monitor	6
Destroyers	16
Torpedo Boats	27
Submarines	8
Steel Gunboats	29
Auxiliaries	26
Screw Steamers	9
Screw Sloops	2
Gunboats	22
Steel Navy	142
Old Navy	33
Total Active	175

The numbers radically changed during the 5 year period from 1898. As indicated above, several new categories were added or eliminated as the U.S. Navy became more modern in their fleet.

December 1909

Battleships	25
Cruisers	27
Monitor	2
Destroyers	20
Torpedo Boats	33
Submarines	16
Steel Gunboats	19
Auxiliaries	29
Gunboats	16
Total Active	187

But a larger Navy also meant a larger cost. In an article published on May 27, 1906 in the *New York Times*, titled "Naval Budget Increased," a naval appropriation bill was going before the United States Senate that provided monies for a "battleship of the type of the Dreadnaught," that would be similar to a vessel being built at the time for the British Royal Navy. An additional one million dollars was appropriated for submarine torpedo boats. To provide for a "reserve supply of powder and shell," an increase was made from one million dollars to two million three hundred thousand dollars, and "for the purchase and manufacture of reserve funds for ships," the appropriation was increased from $500,000 to $750,000" dollars. Last but not least, for extension of the "wireless telegraph systems on the Pacific coast," an additional sixty-five thousand dollars was allocated.

In a further review of increased naval costs, in an article published prior to the First World War on September 4, 1915 in the Fort Wayne Journal-Gazette, titled "The Cost of the Army and Navy" by Clyde H. Tavenner, he stated that the "increase in the cost of our Army and Navy in the last 28 years is enough to stagger the imagination and bewilder the sense." He was quick to point out that it was not "abnormal when considered to the proportion to the increase in our population." To further illustrate his point, the following chart was included in the article. The dollar values indicate the total cost of the Army and Navy during those years.

Year		
	1883	14,903,559
	1889	58,098,787
	1903	78,856,363
	1909	122,662,485
	1914	140,713,434

In an interesting view of the ever-expanding role of the United States Navy, the following numbers illustrate the U.S. Naval Fleet as of the United States involvement in World War One.

November 11, 1918

Battleships	39
Monitors (coastal)	7
Cruisers	31
Destroyers	110
Frigates	17
Submarines	80
Mine warfare	53

Patrol Boats   350
Auxiliary 87
Surface Warships   204

Total Active   774

The total numbers of Ship Force Levels on VJ Day or Victory in Japan Day, August 14, 1945, was when the United States Navy was its height in sheer numbers of vessels in its fleet.

Battleships   23
Carriers (fleet)   28
Carriers (escort) 71
Cruisers   70
Destroyers   377
Frigates   361
Submarines   232
Mine Warfare   586
Patrol   1204
Amphibious   2547
Auxiliary   1267
Surface Warships   833

Total Active   6768

However, a sobering view of the Ship Force Levels occurs when one looks at the number of active vessels as of June 30, 1946. After the end of World War II, the fleet shrank to 1248 vessels. By June 30, 1950, the number would shrink again to a lowly 634 vessels which was less then the active force level in November of 1918. These numbers would of course increase during the Korean and Vietnam conflicts, however as seen previously, the surge was followed by a down swell of activity. A dramatic fall in total ship numbers occurred in 1968-69 as the United States Navy began decommissioning many World War II-era ships.

To provide a historical look, the following numbers reflect the United States Active Ship Levels from November 16, 2001

Battleships   0
Carriers   12
Cruisers   27
Destroyers   54
Frigates   35
Submarines   54
SSBN's   18
Mine Warfare   27
Patrol   13
Amphibious   39
Auxiliary   58
Surface Warships   116

Total Active   337

Appendix D - John Paul Jones – Hero Unwanted?

John Paul Jones' l last offer for a commission from the United States did not arrive in time for him to accept or deny. As thirteen prisoners languished in an Algerian prison, President George Washington and Secretary of State Thomas Jefferson sent John Paul Jones a letter appointing him the "commissioner with full power to negotiate with the Dey of Algiers," according to Samuel Eliot Morison's *John Paul Jones, A Sailors Biography*, page 403. Jones would have probably accepted the position of counsel to Algiers, but the letter was sent to France under courier of Thomas Pickney and the ship in which he traveled upon would arrive too late. Jones would not know of his last call to service of the United States as he would instead answer the call of mortality.

Consul to Algiers would have been another title that John Paul Jones would have had to include in the long line of his accomplishments, heroics, positions, and duties. Born in Scotland, John Paul led an adventurous and storied life that included, according to a biographical sketch reprinted in S. Putnam Waldo Esq.'s text, *Biographical Sketches of Distinguished American Naval Heroes in the War of the Revolution*, page 76-77, "commander and Post Captain in the Continental Navy, a prince of smugglers, a gentleman landlord, and grand smuggler." In addition, after his service to the struggling United States, John Paul Jones would also be known as Kontradmiral Pavel Ivanovich Jones or Rear Admiral. But his life was more then just titles and positions. It was rather an adventure through various employments, battles, wars, and courtships. Ultimately however, even for all of his heroics and victories, John Paul Jones would pass from this world a lonely soul.

But how could a man so regarded and respected, on both sides of the Atlantic, sail off into the twilight? Why did he not rise to the forefront of naval leadership in the United States or in another country for that matter? Was it that John Paul Jones was a bastard, a womanizer, and an egotist? Was it because he was a lone wolf who demanded perfection and ran a tight ship? Was he the

American version of Nelson or was he rather a man who fought valiantly on the churning seas of the American Revolution and yet failed to sail smoothly in the turbid political waters of the Department of the Navy?

The true question remains whether or not John Paul Jones was an unwanted hero? It is hard to believe that the naval hero of the American Revolution would not rise to flag rank in the United States after having been victorious in numerous battles having had displayed and epitomized the type of "man" that the United States possessed. But this is exactly what happened. Though decorated by other countries and even requested to provide them military leadership, John Paul Jones was not even promoted to flag rank in the navy in which he had so proudly and gallantly served.

As a hero of the American Revolution, John Paul Jones attempted to persuade the leadership of the United States to invest in a strong navy. But the United States Navy of the era was as Eugene Armbruster reflects upon in his book, *The Wallabout Prison Ships 1776-1783*, on pages 5-7, was rather a "branch of government having exercised through the whole war by committees and boards" only. At one point the United States Congress listened to Jones' reflections and demands for a stronger United States Navy. In light of his actions and leadership under the pressure of battle, a committee was gathered to review the senior officers who would take command of the largest of the United States' ships, the America. As the congressional committee's thoughts of making him Admiral Jones filtered in various political circles, other naval officers began a campaign against him. Ultimately, Jones was scuttled by his own contemporaries who did not wish to see a man less their senior be named to the highest naval rank of the time. And so John Paul Jones remained a Captain and retained with those golden stripes, a vengeful contempt for his brethren and adopted country, the United States.

John Paul Jones left the United States after collecting part of the prize money due him from his efforts during the Revolutionary War. In Paris, Jones was treated as a celebrity in the royal court. He was often asked to retell of his naval battle exploits and he reveled in the ability to do so. In addition, Jones also became friendly with the ladies of the court as well. But action and command of a vessel at sea was his true desire. To lament on land was not his wish.

A call to service came soon after, but it was not from the United States. Instead the offer came from Russia. Empress Catherine II wanted John Paul Jones to command her naval fleet in the Black Sea. But even when he was offered the position, John Paul Jones withdrew his bitter sentiment and sent a letter to Thomas Jefferson requesting that he attempt to influence Congress so that he might be retroactively made Rear Admiral, USN, instead. Even though Jones had been the hero of Flamborough Head, site of the famous battle between his ship the *Bonhomme Richard* and the British *Serapis*, eloquently recorded in print displayed on page 278 of John Grafton's book, *The American Revolution, A Picture Sourcebook*, Jones did not have much of a chance to attain flag rank in a country that had no formal navy. Instead, Jones accepted the position as Rear Admiral in the Russian navy.

But this position would only spell disaster to Jones. During the action in the Black Sea, as Russia battled Crimea, he was not in complete command. As this was not in keeping with his most effective manner of leadership he sounded out against his superiors and was subsequently relieved of his command. Though he had made Rear Admiral the difficulties of political dealings ended his career in the Russian Court. Once again, John Paul Jones' inability to appease and effectively interact with political circles would prove to be his demise.

Jones' life after his Russian command would be limited in activity. Though he wished for the ability to captain a vessel or command a squadron, neither opportunity ever availed itself. Though his time in Russia had been limited, he wished that he could attain some sort of imperial post in the country, but that too would never amount to fruition. He wrote several letters to some of his friends in the United States which displayed a high probability of return to the

Philadelphia area, but he remained in Europe instead. He hoped for a call to duty, a call to the sea, a call to his calling. Unfortunately, the call to serve would not arrive in time.

Jones would pass away and be buried with little pomp and circumstance in France. Many years later, John Paul Jones would finally return to the United States to be laid to rest in the crypt of the United States Naval Academy's chapel. Though it took an inordinate amount of time (he arrived in 1905), he was finally entombed in a marble sarcophagus on January 26, 1913. John Paul Jones, naval hero of the American Revolution and proponent of a strong United States Navy had finally returned home to his adopted country. Though praised and exalted by all upon his return and subsequent entombment in the Les Invalides inspired tomb, there were still those who poked fun at the naval hero. The "old man" of the United States Navy would still have to hear the wise cracks of the midshipmen at Annapolis as they sang a parody of the song "Everybody Works But Father." The lyrics of course, were changed to reflect that everybody, most especially the middies, at the academy had to work but not the poor old pickled John Paul Jones.

John Paul Jones, however he is remembered whether as hero of Flamborough Head, Commodore, Captain or Kontradmiral, he will most importantly be revered by most as one of the most influential naval heroes of all time. His determination, skill, foresight, and actions made him a respected man in both his lifetime and to this day. Though he may not have impressed as many political members of the world as he did the ladies of his time, John Paul Jones' legacy remains apparent. He demanded a strong navy, a military presence on the seas and oceans, and displayed the need for heroic actions during time of battle. These attributes live strong in the officers and petty officers of the naval ranks that serve our country today as it is those young men and woman who stand in the heat of battle and declare "I have not yet begun to fight."

During his short life, John Paul Jones answered to only one call and that call was to the sea. Not a man to answer to his superiors or to the sometimes apparent impending defeat or challenge, Jones was indeed a hero. He embodied the determination and resolve necessary to stare his own fate and destiny in the face and challenge it head on. Hero yes, but to himself as he lamented in a sickly condition, he must have longed to have the ability to spend those last days pondering his loneliness and solitary state. But ultimately, I feel, he must have longed for one last call to service and most importantly one last call to command a "fast ship" setting out to sea for his last twilight patrol.

Suggested Reading & For Further Information

Admirals of American Empire by Richard S. West, Jr.

American Naval History – An Illustrated Chronology of the U.S. Navy and Marine Corps, 1775 – Present by Jack Sweetman

Creative History – An Introduction to Historical Study by Walter T.K. Nugent

Navies in History by Clark G. Reynolds

Peter Freuchen's Book of the Seven Seas by Peter Freuchen

T.R. - The Last Romantic by H.W. Brands

The Influence of Sea Power Upon History 1660-1783 by A.T. Mahan

The Naval War of 1812 by Theodore Roosevelt

The Rise of Theodore Roosevelt by Edmund Morris

Theodore Rex by Edmund Morris

Theodore Roosevelt by Louis Auchincloss

Theodore Roosevelt by Henry F. Pringle

Theodore Roosevelt – Many-sided American by Naylor, Brinkley and Gable

Theodore Roosevelt's Naval Diplomacy – Cdr. Henry J. Hendrix, USN

This People's Navy by Kenneth J. Hagan

Organizations

The Navy League – www.navyleague.org
Theodore Roosevelt Association – www.tra.org
The Friends of Sagamore Hill – www.Sagamore-Hill.com
United States Navy – www.navy.mil

Index

Underwater Historical Research Society

The Underwater Historical Research Society was co-founded in the winter of 2004 by Adam M. Grohman and Andy Campbell. The main purpose of the society is to research and document underwater wrecks and sites and to educate the public about the rich maritime history that is right below the surface. The Society's membership is open to the general public. The UHRS Dive team is comprised of a select group of divers but based on upcoming projects, additional divers may be needed.

Proceeds from the sale of books, films, and assorted paraphernalia fund upcoming projects. To become a supporting member of the society, visit www.uhrs.org. The Underwater Historical Research Society publishes a quarterly journal that includes research articles, updates on current projects, and other important information regarding the society's activities. Support from memberships allows the society to continue its important historical research.

Members of the Underwater Historical Research Society also facilitate and provide lectures to various organizations, school groups, diving clubs, and other historical societies to further promote the important maritime history of local and surrounding waters.

To receive more information regarding the Underwater Historical Research Society, to request a complimentary copy of In-Depth, the society's quarterly journal, or to simply let us know your thoughts, please feel free to visit our website at www.uhrs.org or via regular mail at our offices. Thank you.

Mailing Address: Underwater Historical Research Society
Attn: Adam Grohman
P.O. Box 78
Locust Valley, NY 11560

About the Author

Adam Matthew Grohman was born and raised in Pomona, New Jersey. He received his Associates in Science and Associates in Arts from Atlantic Cape Community College and then went to Long Island University at C.W. Post and completed his Bachelor's in Fine Arts degree in Film. He recently completed his Master's in Arts in American History from American Military University. He is a boatswain's mate in the United States Coast Guard Reserve and has served in Cape May, New Jersey, San Diego, California, Guantanamo Bay, Cuba as a member of a USCG Port Security Unit Detachment, and most recently, Jones Beach, New York. Adam is a PADI Dive Master and has successfully researched multiple shipwrecks and their histories in the New York and Long Island areas. His columns, "In Our Waters" and "Sentinels and Saviors of the Seas" – which highlights the rich history of the United States Coast Guard - are featured monthly in *Long Island Boating World* Magazine. Adam, Kendall, and their two sons Aidan and Liam live in Long Island, New York.

Also by Adam Grohman

Non Fiction

Non Liquet - The Bayville Submarine Mystery
Runner Aground - A History of the Schooner *William T. Bell*
Ugly Duckling - Liberty Ship *S.S. C.W. Post*
Mask, Fins & Knife - A History of the U.S. Navy UDT & SEAL Diving Equipment from World War II to Present
Beneath the Blue & Gray Waves - Sub-Marine Warfare of the American Civil War
Claimed by the Sea - Long Island Shipwrecks
Dive GTMO - Scuba Diving in Guantanamo Bay, Cuba (co-author Andy Campbell)

Fiction

A Bright Shining Light
Surfer Girl – A Love Story

The following titles may be ordered by visiting www.uhrs.org